A WHITE MAN'S

一个白人的中国

A WHITE MAN'S

一个白人的中国

GEORGE JAEGGI

乔治雅阁

CITIOFBOOKS, INC.
3736 Eubank NE Suite A1
Albuquerque, NM 87111-3579
www.citiofbooks.com
Hotline: 1 (877) 389-2759
Fax: 1 (505) 930-7244

Ordering Information:

Quantity sales. Special discounts are available on quantity purchases by corporations, associations, and others. For details, contact the publisher at the address above.

Printed in the United States of America.

ISBN-13:   Softcover   979-8-89391-537-2
                  eBook   979-8-89391-538-9

Library of Congress Control Number: 2025902793

Table of Contents

Table of Contents

PART 2

DEDICATION

This book is dedicated to all of you reading my thoughts about my China experiences.

I have met many people over my lifetime and each of them has given me some insight into what this world is all about and made me appreciate the title of the 1966 Clint Eastwood movie: The Good, The Bad and The Ugly.

I am grateful for the patience and understanding of all my family, my wife Kim, my daughter Christine and her family, my son Brian and his family, and my four grandsons, Henry, Mason, Charlie, and Jordan. I would like to thank all my friends who encouraged me to write this book, and I hope you will enjoy the awkward ways of my worldview.

ACKNOWLEDGEMENTS

Writing this book about my journeys to China has been a rewarding experience for me and it has made me aware of the many difficulties I encountered over my last 18 years. I have many people to thank for their encouragement that gave me the will and strength to complete this book. I express my deepest appreciation to my wife, Kim, my daughter Christine, and my son Brian for accepting and supporting me in my solitude while writing and rewriting my thoughts over and over.

However, nothing would have been achieved without all the people I met in my 50-plus journeys, and I like to thank and mention some of them, mainly using their English or Chinese first names only. Most of my Chinese friends with Englishgiven names have picked out their English names themselves to integrate better with foreigners. I like to acknowledge my earliest contacts who have helped me to overcome my initial awkwardness and who have encouraged me to understand and appreciate the Chinese way of life: Special thanks to Joan W., Yang L., Marcus H., Alex, Annie, David, Machell, Andy, Bruce, Dong, Mark P. and all my WeChat friends Philip, Jeff, Austin, George G., Sandy, Boming, Angela, Omia, Susan, Paul, Jim, Charles, Szilveszter, Imre, Marion, Xin, Zhu, Curtis, Vinzzy, Marc Z. and many more….and you all know who you are and what you have contributed to my writing, The name of the book was a combination of remarks and suggestions made by many of you. You kept telling me that I should call the book "A White Man's China," as I was a white man in China who had the chance to discover a China that most white people will never get to know or understand. Many of you also kept encouraging me to write the book in a very simple fashion, which the readers can easily understand. It will encourage my Chinese friends to appreciate how a white man looks at China and how the Chinese appear to total strangers. You all have helped me to bridge the gap between our diverse cultures, and I am very grateful for all your encouragement and understanding.

I would also like to express my gratitude to the Citi of Books team for their guidance throughout the publishing and marketing process. A special thanks to Chloe Bennett, Elle Sanchez, and everyone in the marketing team, as well as Derrick Hogan and Rick Wallace.

Part 1

My unique personal experiences in China

How I discovered a China which was not the China I thought I knew

THE CHINA I DISCOVERED

Why China? I have been asked this question by many of my friends and general acquaintance. The only answer I can give them is that I feel it is important to hear my stories as a naïve business entrepreneur who traveled to China based on what I had read and was told by consultants. I thought I knew all about China, and then came the realization of how naïve I was when the "real" China was in front of me.

Many years ago, a very successful business friend told me that **reading and dreaming about anything you want to do is great, but if you are serious about anything new, there is only one way to succeed**. GO THERE AND SEE FOR YOURSELF!

I realize now that successful consultants are basic salesmen who are great at their jobs and can sell and describe a side of the business their clients are looking for. The one problem is that most consultants do not understand the depth of your business needs, and they will easily convince you that everything is readily achievable. They have a network of business associates and will outsource business dealings to their friends, and in the end, they will take no responsibility for the outcome of their advice.

If money is no issue in your business, consultants are the way to go as long you give them directions on what you expect to be achieved. **However, if you are a hands-on entrepreneur and money does not grow on trees in your backyard, you must be clear about your objectives** and pick and choose your path forward.

In my writings, you will discover the many mistakes and setbacks I experienced in my early travels and business dealings in China. Then you will also discover how **setbacks can educate you and give you the know-how and confidence to succeed.**

While in China on business, I also took the opportunity to travel to many parts of China and get to know the many different ways of life of ordinary Chinese. I was in many touristy areas, but I also was able to visit places in China where I could spend days without meeting a Westerner, and I was able to get to know some aspects of ordinary life, including getting to appreciate the local foods in each region. Talking about Chinese food makes me smile. When people ask me if I like Chinese food, I usually ask them what they consider Chinese food. There are many unique Chinese dishes from each area in China, and most cities and provinces have their dishes. The locals are proud of their food and happy when they see that foreigners also like their specialities. For example, a

Westerner is most likely familiar with Cantonese, Szechuan, or Hunan Chinese food; however, Shanghainese consider Cantonese food as Western food and insist that only Shanghainese food is real Chinese food. However, traveling up North to Jiangsu, Dalian, or Jilin, you will find different speciality dishes. I tell people that I love all kinds of Chinese food, as long nothing moves after I do the shake test, and I will explain later about the shake test.

And I want to clarify one thing: **I am not an expert on China**, and I am not here to tell you that I know China. **I simply want to tell you my experiences while visiting China during the last 18 years and over 50 trips** to China and spending 2 to 3 weeks each time in various places.

I have many friends on WeChat, and many of my Chinese friends have encouraged me to tell my story and possibly have my book translated into Mandarin. I was told that Chinese people are also very interested to know how Westerners feel about China. It will let them appreciate and make them understand why we act in such strange ways when we encounter different situations in China.

BUT WHY WRITE A BOOK ABOUT CHINA?

Growing up in Switzerland just after the end of WW2, we uniquely looked at history compared to most other countries. Switzerland was a neutral country during the war; However, there were many opinions about the beginning and end of WW2. It was a confusing time, depending on what you read or heard from family and teachers. There was no internet or Google, and information was mostly word of mouth, and newspapers would print information way after the fact. So, of course, everyone had an opinion, and there was no use trying to convince someone to be open-minded as there was no way to prove any assumption you may have believed to be true.

As a Swiss, it was natural to feel privileged and a little conceded about anything you heard about how and why the war ended. History (as I see it as "His Story") entirely depends on who tells you "His Story." As I grew older, the schoolbooks were full of stories about WW2, and one was guided to believe that the good won over the bad. **The world started progressing in every direction, and new and unexpected alliances were formed.**

Being interested in history and geography, I read and studied a lot about foreign countries and their past and current standing. **I was fascinated by the empires and dynasties of the past and their influence on today's world.** I realized that empires and dynasties are great while they lasted, but like everything in this world, they only lasted that long, and then a new era started and the "old" moved on, and they tried to live off the past glory. So, I read books and studied the geographical maps of China. I thought I knew what China was all about. However, I also realized that China was a closed country to the outside world in the sixties, especially the Western world, but times changed. By the year 2005, my situation prompted me and the company I was working for to go to China to find a way to keep the manufacturing business competitive and expand the reach of the current customers.

But why write about China? I have been asked this question many times, and I realize there are plenty of books written about China. However, my outlook and my way of looking at China will help many people to understand and appreciate what China has to offer. I will always avoid political rhetoric and tell you my opinion. **China will be one of the next Superpowers in our universe,** and the best way to benefit is to participate in building the new world structure. It is like surfing and riding a strong wave in the ocean, and if you're on top of the wave, you are safe, but if you're at the wrong end, you are either stuck or you might get crushed. **I am not here to tell anyone what to do and how to do it,** but I like to tell you my experiences from my first visit to China in 2005, and then the over 50 trips and over 800 days in many different parts of China. I have experienced most of the touristy parts of China, but more importantly, I have experienced many nontouristy areas and observed the everyday lives of ordinary Chinese people. **I am not saying that there is anything wrong with the touristy areas, but to be real, you must realize that mostly it is a show to the world, the way they want you to see China.**

China's size and vast population

When I was born **in 1950, the world population was around 2.5 billion; in 2020, it just reached 7.8 billion.** China's population in 1950 was about 550 million, and in 2020 over 1.4 billion. The Swiss population in 1950 was 4.6 million, and in 2020, 8.6 million; the US population in 1950 was 151 million; by 2020, it was around 335 million. This population growth is phenomenal, and it leads to a changed way of life in every aspect, from food and goods supplies to manufacturing processes to climate changes and the use of fossil fuels and electricity sources for power generation.

The first Mainland Chinese city I visited was Xiamen in the Fujian Province. Our Xiamen contact had arranged to attend a business exhibition in Shanghai, and he said we also would see a potential supplier in Ningbo. I had never heard of Ningbo before. I looked it up on a map and realized it is a city of over 8 million people. You tell me of any city in the Western world of 8 million people, and you would not know their name. **I was told that there were over 84 cities in China with a population of over 1 million.** We then went on to Shanghai, and the population of Shanghai were around 25 million. That is then when you start realizing the vast power hidden in China.

The size of the economy and the power of growth potential is enormous. It can lead to unpredictable success for whoever provides guidance and patience.

HISTORY LESSON AND APPRECIATION OF THE PAST CHINESE CULTURE

While looking into China's history, I went back to my high school history books and looked at the notes I had made about China during our history lessons. I was always fascinated by Empires and Dynasties. I did a lot of reading about empires from the Egyptian Empire (1550 BC -1077 BC), Roman Empire (501 BC -1453 AD), Byzantine Empire (395-1453), Ottoman Empire (1299-1922), British Empire (1603-1947) and many others, like the Russian Empire, the French, the Dutch, Portuguese and German. Traveling and appreciating the Chinese culture. I started enjoying the history of China, past and present. In our fast-moving world, we can easily forget the past and how many achievements shaped our world. Following is a list of the Chinese Dynasties as I know them and the way I was taught. **History books have many stories about the 3982 Years of Dynasties and Empires and the many Emperors and their achievements. From the Xia Dynasty starting in 2070 BC to the Qing Dynasty ending in 1912.**

Xia Dynasty (2070–1600 BC): The Xia Dynasty was considered the first dynasty of ancient China to live alongside the Yellow River and is regarded as the beginning of China's hereditary dynasty.

Shang Dynasty (1600–1046 BC): Chinese civilization began along the Yellow River in the Shang era and represented the earliest form of Chinese writing.

Zhou Dynasty (1045-221 BC): Major philosophies, such as Confucianism and Daoism, emerged. **Also, during this period lived the legendary military strategist Sun Zi and his philosophies about war, published in the book "The Art of War."**

Qin Dynasty (221–206 BC): The Qin Dynasty was the first to unite China as a country under an emperor and was the shortest dynasty in

China, lasting only 15 years. The First Emperor— Qin Shi Huang was the first emperor to use the title of emperor in China. He standardized units of weight and measurements, as well as the writing system. In addition, great building projects, such as the Great Wall and the Terracotta Army, were built based on this system.

The Han Dynasty (206 BC – 220 AD): The Han Dynasty existed at the same time as the Roman Empire. It started the Silk Road that connected China with Central Asia and Europe. Confucianism was officially elevated to orthodox status. Buddhism, originating in ancient India, was introduced to China, and Taoism, China's local religion, arose.

Hua Tuo invented the first anaesthetic and was the first doctor in the world to operate under general anaesthesia. Cai Lun improved the technique of paper making, and Zhang Heng invented a seismograph that could measure earthquakes.

Wei, Jin, the Southern, and Northern Dynasties (220– 581): When the Han Dynasty fell into decline, this period saw the **most frequent regime changes in** Chinese history. During this period, other ethnicities in the north established political power and moved to the central plains, gradually accepting the Han culture. **National integration** reached its climax. **Buddhism was widespread, and** the rulers used Buddhist ideas to encourage the people to put their hope in the afterlife.

The Sui Dynasty (581–618): The Sui Dynasty was intense, with **great conquests and achievements**, such as the Grand Canal and the rebuilding of the Great Wall.

The Tang Dynasty (618-907): During the Tang Dynasty, China emerged as one of the most powerful countries in the world, and its capital Chang'an (now Xi'an), was then one of the largest cities in the world. The second emperor of Tang, Li Shimin, was one of the most extraordinary emperors in Chinese history. In addition, the Tang Dynasty produced the **only female emperor in Chinese history, Wu Zetian.** The Tang Dynasty was the golden age for poetry, painting, tricolored glazed pottery, and woodblock printing. Great Tang poets included Li Bai and Du Fu. China's papermaking, textiles, and other technologies spread to West Asia, Europe, and the Arab region. Islam was introduced to China.

The Song Dynasty (960–1279): The Song Dynasty saw high levels of growth in the commodities economy, culture, education, and scientific innovation in Chinese history. The shipbuilding industry was developed to a high level. Overseas trade was prosperous, communicating with the South Pacific, the Middle East, Africa, and Europe. The "four great inventions" of the Chinese people in ancient times (paper, printing, the compass, and gunpowder) were further developed in the Song Dynasty.

The Yuan Dynasty (1271–1368): Mongol tribes ruled the Yuan Dynasty. Trade, technological development, and China's interaction with foreign countries continued under Mongol rule. During this time, Marco Polo traveled extensively in China.

The Ming Dynasty (1368–1644): The founder, Zhu Yuanzhang, ousted the Mongol Empire in China and began the Ming Dynasty. The Forbidden City was built, and it became the emperor's residence for the remainder of the imperial era.

The Qing Dynasty (1644–1912): The Qing Dynasty was the last imperial dynasty in China's history. Emperor Kangxi and Emperor Qianlong were the two most famous emperors of the Qing Dynasty. Their reigns were "the golden age of prosperity." Modern China's territory was established during this era.

THE NEW CHINA AFTER THE EMPIRES

The Republic of China Era (1912–1949)

The Republican Revolution of 1911, led by **Sun Yat-sen**, ended the rule of the Qing Dynasty. In **1912,** after the collapse of the Qing Dynasty, **China declared itself a Republic with Sun Yat-sen as the first president, and he founded the Nationalist Party, Kuomintang (KMT).**

July 1921 - The Chinese Communist Party (CCP) is founded at the French Concession area in Shanghai with Mao Zedong and Zhou Enlai part of the founders of the Chinese Communist Party.

1925 - Sun Yat-sen died, and Chiang Kai-shek assumed leadership of KMT and launched the Northern Expedition that reunified China under a Nationalist government.

December 1937 - March 1938, The Sino-Japanese War: A fourmonth Japanese occupation of Nanking known as the Rape of Nanking was the cause of an estimated 260,000 Chinese civilian casualties during the invasion.

1946-49 - Civil war between the Nationalists and the Communists resulted in the Communists' victory. The Nationalist government, with its leader Chiang Kai-Shek, evacuated to the island of Taiwan, where Chiang Kai-Shek remained the leader of the Nationalist government until he died in 1975.

Modern China (1949–now) - In 1949, on October 1, Mao Zedong declared the PCR the People's Republic of China and entered a Communist era of stability. Chairman Mao named Zhou Enlai as its first premier.

On February 21, 1972, US President Richard Nixon made a historic visit to China, meeting with Chairman Mao Zedong and Premier Zhou Enlai, establishing diplomatic relations between the two countries, ending twenty-five years of isolation between the United States of America and the People's Republic of China (PCR).

In 1976, following Mao's death, Deng Xiaoping outmaneuvered the late chairman's chosen successor Hua Guofeng and became the de facto top leader of the Communist Party of China (CPC). Under his leadership, he brought forward the Reforms and Opening-up policy of 1978, bringing China phenomenal economic growth.

In 1987, Western-style fast food was introduced in China— KFC opened its first store, and McDonald's followed shortly after.

In 1990, China's most extensive notable economic zone was launched in the suburbs of Shanghai at Pudong, designed to be China's Financial and Commercial Centre.

In 2001, China was admitted to the World Trade Organization and won the bid for the 2008 Olympics and the 2008 Summer Olympics in Beijing.

APPRECIATION OF THE MANY CHINESE CITIES I VISITED

The majority of Westerners have an outdated and inaccurate view of China

They read in their newspapers and magazines about China being a mysterious, unknown faraway giant, which arouses distrust and even fears.

"Made in China" seems to be the most common phrase, but if you want to do business in China, think of "Made for China" and accept and adapt to the cultural differences between your way of thinking and the Chinese way of life.

Communication is the key, and understanding the cultural differences within China is more important than what any China expert can tell you. What works in Shanghai may not work in Beijing and certainly will be different in Jilin, Xiamen, or Shenzhen. When I say works, I mean how you approach a business start-up and negotiate with local government officials.

Each area of China has its characteristics, and you need to get a feel for each area and adapt your thinking accordingly. China is known for its architectural wonders, such as the Great Wall and Forbidden City, its staggering variety of delicious food and martial arts, and its long history of inventions. More than just tea and temples, China is a fast-changing mix of the ultramodern and the very ancient.

Let's talk about the main cities I visited and point out what they are best known for from a touristy point of view:

Beijing: Forbidden City, Summer Palace, Temple of Heaven, Ming Tombs, and nearby the Great Wall.

Shanghai: The Bund, Nanjing Road, Yu Yuan Garden, People Square, Xintiandi, Pudong, Financial Centre, and many tall buildings, Oriental Pearl Tower.

Tianjin: Tianjin is a coastal metropolis in Northern China on the shore of the Bohai Sea.

Chongqing: Chongqing is a sprawling municipality in southwestern China's confluence of the Yangtze and Jialing rivers. The large, domed Great Hall of the People complex stands in the city center, above People's Square.

Harbin: Harbin, whose name was originally a Manchu word, grew from a small rural settlement on the Songhua River to one of the largest cities in Northeast China, and it's known for its ice sculpture festival in the winter.

Shandong: Shandong, an eastern Chinese province on the Yellow Sea, is known for its Taoist and Confucian heritage. Shandong is known as the birthplace of Confucius.

Qingdao: Qingdao is well known for its beer, a legacy of the German occupation between 1898 to 1914. The Tsingtao Beer Museum celebrates the namesake brewery, founded by Germans in 1903.

Changchun: Situated in Northeast China's Jilin province. In February 1991, FAW-Volkswagen Corporation Ltd. was established in Changchun, creating the Volkswagen Group's second joint venture in China after Shanghai, which was established in 1984.

Dalian: Dalian is a modern port city on the Liaodong Peninsula. It was founded in 1898 by Russia, and there are many Russian-style architectural buildings. Zhongshan Square has colonial buildings in the Renaissance style.

Shenyang: Shenyang is the capital of Liaoning Province and is the bridge between North Korea and the outside world.

Jiangsu: Jiangsu is a coastal Chinese province north of Shanghai.

Nanjing: Situated in the Yangtze River Delta region, Nanjing has a prominent place in Chinese history and culture, having served as the capital of various Chinese dynasties, kingdoms, and republican governments dating from the 3rd century to 1949.

Yancheng: Yancheng City is a major coastal city in the Jiangsu Province.

Suzhou is renowned for its elaborate gardens. These include the Humble Administrator's Garden, its network of pools linked by pagodas and pavilions, and the Lion Grove Garden.

Hangzhou, Western Lake

I love this Ancient Chinese poem:

"In heaven there is paradise; on earth there is Suzhou and Hangzhou." Even Marco Polo called it the "most beautiful and magnificent city."

Hangzhou has a history of mysterious stories from the past and the West Lake is known for the phrase.

"Forged from the Battles of Heaven."

Hangzhou Bay Bridge: 35.6 Km in length, this bridge shortened the journey from Shanghai to Ningbo from 400 Km to 180 Km and reduced travel time from 4 to about 2 hours. It opened for public use in 2008. At the center of the bridge is a Service Centre with a hotel and shopping center.

Guangdong: borders Hong Kong and is famous for their Cantonese cuisine

Guilin: Guilin is a tourist destination in Guangxi province in southern China, known for its fascinating landscape of limestone karst hills and caves. At its center are two lakes, and boats travel through these and other lakes via connected rivers.

Great Wall: The Great Wall is a popular tourist destination. The site of the most visited section of the Great Wall is near the 4th tower at Badaling.

Xi'an: It's the capital of Shaanxi Province in central China. It marked the eastern end of the Silk Road and was the capital and home of several ruling dynasties. There is an archaeological site in Xi'an's surrounding plains known as the Terra Cotta Army, where thousands of life-size and handmolded figurines are buried.

Hefei: It's the capital and cultural center of the Anhui Province.

Chengdu: It's famous for the Giant Panda Breeding Base, and the conservation center is a great place to view the endangered giant pandas in a natural habitat. Chengdu is the capital of the southwestern Sichuan province, and its cuisine is well known for its spicy taste.

Changsha: Regarding spicy food, Changsha is the capital of Hunan, and its red peppers will make any meal as hot as possible. The Hunan region is Mao's early home, born in 1893. In the village of Shaoshan is a mud-brick house where Mao was born, and there is now the Mao Zedong Memorial Museum.

Xiamen: Xiamen, also known as Amoy, is in the Fujian Province and was a British-run treaty port from 1842 to 1912. Xiamen and the beautiful touristy Gulangyu Island are less than 6 km from Taiwan.

Shenzhen: Shenzhen is next to Hong Kong, separated by a narrow winding river. Shenzhen is a global center in technology, research, and manufacturing, and the port of Shenzhen is one of the world's busiest container ports.

Sanya on Hainan Island: It's also called the "Hawaii of China" with its beautiful beaches and is a favorite tourist destination for Northern Chinese during the winter months.

Hong Kong: Located east of the Pearl River bordering the Guangdong province to the North and the South China Sea east, south, and west. Hong Kong is a Special Administrative Region of the People's Republic of China (PRC).

Macao: Macao is across the Pearl River Delta from Hong Kong. It was a Portuguese territory until 1999, and it reflects a mix of cultural influences and is best known for its giant casinos and malls. The Cotai Strip has earned its nickname "Las Vegas of Asia."

When talking to your Chinese friends, **you will hear many sayings, and they could stem from Confucius to Tao to Mao**. Many sayings are based on Buddhism or any other Chinese philosophy, but the most crucial part is the **fact that you must try to understand the wisdom behind those sayings.**

This following quote from Sun Zi, the Chinese military general and philosopher, is taught in Chinese schools from an early age. As a result, his thinking plays a vital role in Chinese political and economic strategies.

The one who knows himself and knows the other

can fight a hundred battles and win a hundred victories

Sun Zi, The Art of War, 5th century BC

HOW SAFE IS IT TO BE A WESTERNER IN CHINA?

As I mentioned, I have been to China over 50 times and spent over 800 days in many different places, from 5-star hotels to no-star locations in many other cities and provinces. **I often spent a few days in areas without meeting a Westerner.** I preferred to spend time in different non-touristy places and my business associates and suppliers would arrange for me to visit their hometowns. They would arrange for someone to pick me up from the airport or bus terminal and bring me to a nearby hotel. During the day, someone would take me around and show me their unique places in their towns, and evenings would be spent at a dinner with their family and friends. At no time did I feel worried or threatened, as ordinary Chinese people are very humble and friendly. **I had young kids point fingers at me and make fun of my looks. Teenagers would walk by and say "Hi" in English and then laugh when I answered, saying "Ni Hao."** I know many Mandarin words, but I cannot speak in sentences or hold a conversation, but when I hear them speak between each other, I can sometimes tell what they are talking about and if the talk is friendly or if they are upset about something. Chinese love to speak loudly, and for us, it can be easily interpreted as hostile. One eventually learns that the loud voices, which sound like yelling when they talk to each other, do not mean they are angry at each other.

Playing card games is a favorite pastime for most Chinese, and luckily, I also love any card game. However, I am horrible at playing Mahjong. Therefore, I also got quickly introduced to many different dice games. **While playing games, language is no problem as long you are willing to mention occasionally the most popular word in China, "Gan Bei" and if all else fails, smile!**

Another popular pastime is Karaoke, but this is mostly with business associates in the larger cities at the local hotels.

Traveling and meeting people with different backgrounds gave me insights into many different ways of life and an understanding of the local priorities and their way of life. When you are in rural and northern areas, you start to appreciate the true nature of how most people live with minimal means. Most people have good-natured personalities open to accepting outsiders without jealousy or envy, knowing very well that the White Man must be of higher standard compared to their existence. However, if you are friendly and treat them respectfully, they appreciate your company and will make you feel welcome.

UNDERSTANDING THE CHINESE WAY OF LIFE

When in China, do as the Chinese do!

This section is helpful to understand even if you're a tourist and not just on business in China. There are basic rules which will be beneficial to know in any situation. But always remember that you should not pretend to know everything about China. Chinese people appreciate it if you try to understand their procedures and always remember that a big happy smile will get you anywhere in China.

Accept and understand the very basics of Chinese Etiquette

Build trust by immersing yourself in Chinese cultural practices and learning to respect and understand the various ancient rituals.

Remember that you don't get a second chance to make an excellent first impression

Greetings: Wait for the Chinese counterpart to offer their hand first for a "Western-style" handshake, and if they don't feel comfortable shaking hands, do not take it as a sign of hostility; nod your head a little.

Meals: Seating arrangements: If you meet with a group of people for dinner, it will most likely be in a separate room with a round table, and you will sit beside your acquaintance the furthest away from the door.

Food: Arranging the food should be left to your Chinese friend or contact, but if the dinner is by your invitation, ensure that you will look after the bill and avoid embarrassing moments. Traditionally, every dish will be presented to you first, and politely help yourself with every dish. Never empty your plate as an empty plate might indicate that there needs to be more food. I also made it a habit to tell which food I am allergic to. It's best not to say that you don't like certain foods, so a medical excuse will be very helpful. However, I have a story about why I do not eat lamb. When I was a little boy growing up in Switzerland, we had a few sheep that we fed until they were ready for the market. One day one sheep gave birth to 2 baby lambs, and she refused to let the one little one have her milk. So I decided to bottle-feed it, and the little lamb became my pet. But as time passed, the little lamb grew to be a large sheep and was ready to be sold on the market. The following Sunday, we had as our main meal roasted lamb and I was told, that this is from my lovely pet lamb. I cried and never ate lamb again. At a business meal in Shanghai, my contact ordered lamb and wanted me to eat and after I told him my story, he mentioned that I could eat this lamb, as it was not my lamb. However, I knew that he was a practising Buddhist and I asked him how he can promise me that this is not my lamb. He looked at me and nodded, and he never asked me to eat lamb again.

Maotai/Toasts: Having a toast before the meal is customary. Each member on your table, other than the designated driver, will come over and offer a toast and, in return, you are expected to visit each one after and offer a toast to them as well. Moatai is a fairly high grade, and you have to be careful not to get too overwhelmed with drinking, but with the main people on your table, you have to do "Gangbei," which means "bottoms-up." However, with the people whom you do not know well, a little sip will do.

Gift exchanges: The best way to offer a gift is to mention it to the person you have a gift for and find out if a presentation at the table or after the meal in the parking lot is more appropriate. If you offer a gift to a person on the table, you might get anguish or jealous looks from others.

Networking-Karaoke: After a nice meal, it is often customary that you will be invited to join the party in a karaoke room and have an enjoyable evening. Don't be shy and participate with at least one song. You will be amazed how the Chinese people love to sing and don't forget to applaud after every song. Some places also offer card or dice games; the more you participate, the more trust you build within your group.

Colors: Red and more red is the most beloved color in China. **Numbers**: Anything with an eight will be lucky.

Dragon: The Dragon will always be the favorite symbol in China.

The art of communication: Talking about traditional

Chinese festivals is a great starting point. Show interest in the achievements of their ancestors and listen to their stories. Then talk about similarities of your Western culture to the Chinese culture.

Chinese Festivals: Always have a Chinese calendar and mark all festivals. The Chinese are always surprised if you mention their celebrations, and they love telling you stories about the origins of their special festivals.

Spring Festival (known as the Chinese New Year) / Lantern Festival / Qing Ming Festival / Duan Wu Festival / Qi Xi Festival / Mid-Autumn Festival / Chong Yang Festival, and there are probably a few more. As mentioned before, a Chinese calendar will be very helpful and your Chinese friends will be impressed if you know the 12 Zodiac animals, starting with the animal you are born into. In my case, **I am a tiger** and then follow the rabbit, dragon, snake, horse, sheep, monkey, rooster, dog, pig, rat, and ox.

General talking points

I forgot to mention that any subject about politics or business is no topic at any dinner. Instead, talk about family and friends and show them your interest in and appreciation of China.

How about learning some essential Mandarin words

As I mentioned, I have visited China over 50 times, but for some reason, I have never been able to converse in Mandarin. I know a lot of words and phrases, but not enough to say that I speak or understand Mandarin. Here are some of the most basic terms:

Ni Hao (hello), Ni Hao Ma ? (how are you?), Zao Shang Hao (good morning).

Zy Jian (Bye), Shi Shie (thank you), Bu, Shi Shie (no, thank you) Bu Ke Tchi (you're welcome) Chi Zao Fan (eat breakfast) Chi Wu Fan (eat lunch) Chi Wan Fan (eat dinner) Mam mam chi (bon appetite) Tscha (tea) Mei YoUonTi (no problem) Mei Yo (never), Dwee-boo-chee (sorry), Ching (please) wo-boo-dong (I don't understand), Ching zy-shuo (excuse me), Fu wu yuan (waiter/waitress) Mai dan (pay bill), Su Shi (right), Zo shi (left), Pu dong (east side), Pu xi (west side) Qiao (bridge) Wo Shi (I am), Ni Shi (you are), Ta Shi (he/she/it is), Wo Men Shi (we are) Ta Men Shi (they are).

Counting 1 to 10…. Yi, Er, San, Si, Wu, Liu, Tchi, Ba, Jiu, Shi.

11 to 20…Shi Yi, Shi Er, Shi San, Shi Si, Shi Wu, Shi Liu, Shi Tchi, Shi Ba, Shi Jiu, Er Shi.

Jin Tien (today), Ming Tien (tomorrow) Xin Qi Yi (Monday), Xin Qi Er (Tuesday), Xin Qi San (Wednesday), Xin Qi Si (Thursday), Xin Qi Wu (Friday), Xin Qi Liu (Saturday), Xin Qi Tien (Sunday).

Xin NianHoa or Xin NianKuaile (Happy New Year) Ganbei (bottoms up or empty cup)

MY EARLY DAYS IN XIAMEN

Always keep in mind that when in China, you are a guest of their country and accept their way of life and do as the Chinese do.

This is good advice, but only if you know what a Chinese would do in your situation. I am used to traveling to many countries in Europe, the USA, and Mexico and I traveled many times alone with just an address of a local hotel, and I had my issues in these countries, however, I was mostly able to communicate with a dictionary in my hand. But when I arrived in 2005 the first time in China it was different than anywhere I had ever been and a dictionary did not help. The one big difference besides the language is the signs. At Beijing's airport, it was a little easier, since there were people who would understand and speak English and some signs were actually in English, but when I arrived in **Xiamen a city in the Fujian Province**, it was total confusion for me. I had the address of the hotel, and I was looking to get a taxi. However, when I showed the driver the address, he did not seem to recognize the address. I found someone who looked very official, and I asked him if he could get me a taxi to get to the hotel. He talked back in Chinese to me and talked to the taxi driver and I was on my way. Once at the hotel, which was a Western hotel, I called my contact, who I was to meet for dinner that day. He was a European who lived in Xiamen for over 10 years, and he laughed when he found out that I never was in China before. Needless to say, he helped me adjust to my new surroundings and the next morning, he came to meet me for breakfast and then took me to the meetings which were arranged to discuss the manufacturing issues for foreigners in China.

Xiamen is a lovely place, and it is also known as Amoy.

One afternoon, I had some free time, and I took a ferry over to **Gulangyu Island** which is a vehicle-free island and you can walk anywhere quite comfortably. It has a touristy shopping area and has, of course, beautiful sandy beaches and many old colonial villas.,

Xiamen, in 2005, had a population of about 2 million and is currently close to 4 million. The Xiamen International Marathon, which began in 2003 and is known as the Gold Label Road Race is famous for its scenic coastal course as the entire race follows the scenic sections of this coastal city. **I often tell people that Xiamen is the San Diego of China, and it makes people who know Xiamen smile.** Xiamen is also closest to Taiwan as Taiwan's Kinmen Island is just 6 Km from the Xiamen coast. A popular tourist destination is a boat ride from Xiamen towards Kinmen Island, and at one point, you are being told that you are now actually in Taiwan territory. The boat is usually filled with mostly Chinese tourists, and they take pictures and more pictures to show to their relatives at home.

I met many interesting people in Xiamen. I was able to visit many local areas including many restaurants. I loved restaurants near the beaches and one place we would hang out was called Me&You2Bar which is located on the seaside in Haiwan Park. Many foreigners would be

there and exchange stories about their experiences. One such story I was made aware of was about the notorious **Lai Changxing** who lived and did business in Xiamen. He started as an illiterate farmer, but in the tumult of China's burgeoning economy became a newly minted billionaire and was considered at one point as the richest Chinese. He was a living legend who eventually ran afoul of authorities. Lai embodies the story of China's recent success as well as its Achilles' heel. He commanded a highly charged economy, blended with the free market, but unfortunately, it was riddled with corruption. During the criminal trial of Lai, we were made aware of a nightclub hostess and her way of doing business at a location called The Red Mansion which was tucked away in an industrial area in Xiamen.

His life story is well documented in a book called Inside the Red Mansion written by Oliver August. I was intrigued by the descriptions of the Red Mansion and I asked my contact if it was possible to visit such an establishment. It was not easy to get access to these kinds of places as they have incredible security and only allow people inside who they know and trust or who are being referred by a regular customer, and of course, they only like customers who are willing to spend a lot of money. My contact knew a waiter there and he told us that he could let us sit by the exit door as long we stayed at our seats, drank our beer, and leave quietly when or if asked to leave. What I was able to observe was exactly the way it was described in Oliver August's book. We stayed for 2 singing shows. Outside of Xiamen is Tongan and there is a replica of the buildings of the Forbidden City, and it's owned by a TV station and used in many Chinese movies and shows. I was in Xiamen many times during the first 2 years, and it was a learning experience to help start up a factory and get to know Chinese engineers and managers, and in general, help and teach new employees the process of our production and our expectations. We had engineers from our home base helping in the beginning until our Chinese management team was able to handle the production and produce to our expectations.

At one time in Xiamen, I also visited an open meat market, and you must have a good stomach to walk through the various meat sections in 30+ Celsius heat.

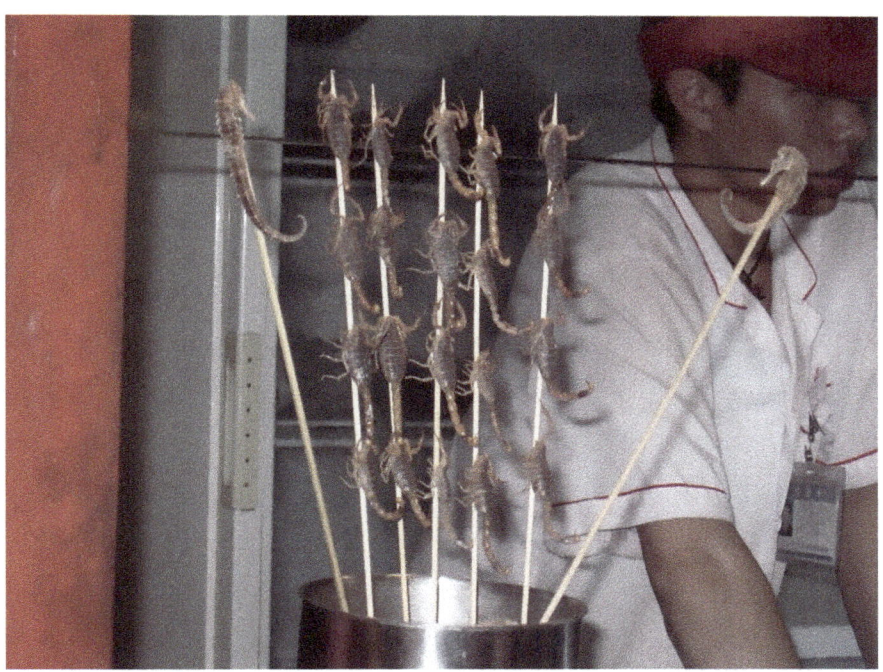

Xiamen remains one of my favorite places I ever visited and got to know.

THE ROUND HOUSES OF THE HAKKA PEOPLE

One weekend, the wife of my contact asked me if I would want to go visit the Round Houses of the Hakka people. I knew nothing about the Hakka people or Round Houses, but I was always up to learning new things and exploring new areas. She arranged a mini-van and she knew the lady driver very well who also understood and talked a little English. She said it will be about a 2-hour ride from Xiamen towards Tulou and we can visit a touristy Round House up in the mountain area towards the interior of the Fujian region. On our way, we drove through many tea and banana plantations. As we approached the touristy Round House, we were greeted by people dressed in beautiful outfits. Many souvenir and tea stalls covered all kinds of trinkets and, of course, lots of tea, as the Fujian province is well known for its tea. The lady driver noticed that we looked a little bored. She asked us if we would rather visit a "real" Round House where "real" people live. She mentioned that her grandmother was living in one of these houses and she mentioned that usually they do not like Westerner visitors, but her grandma will be able to let us visit her at her house. We happily agreed and we arrived there, and I never saw such an amazing structure of a community house. There live about 600 people in this roundhouse, and while the adults go out for work during the day, the elderly take care of the children. We were greeted by many young children and they were amazed to see Westerners. They made fun of our eyes and the color of our hair as the wife from our contact had blond hair and mine was slightly turning grey. We were invited to visit and enter the living rooms and balconies. In the middle of the roundhouse was the general open plaza for the people to gather. There also was a well for their water supply, and I was told that there were fish at the bottom of the well. As long the fish looked healthy, they knew that the water was safe to drink. There were many different animals around, and it was quite an experience to see how they lived, but most of all, to realize how friendly and happy everyone looked.

Inside the Hakka Roundhouse

In 2008, **UNESCO declared** China's Hakka Houses an official World Heritage Site, noting the historic, cultural, and architectural value of these amazing structures. Constructed in the early 12th century, these buildings house up to 600 people each, a city within a city that provided its inhabitants with safety, shelter, and community services. To put this in perspective, I grew up in Halten, Switzerland, in a village of 451 people. Here, in one building, there were over 600 people living. I took many pictures from this special Round House and it remains one of my most memorable experiences in China.

SHANGHAI MY FAVORITE CITY

Shanghai, Oriental Paris: It is China's biggest city with a population of over 25 million and is known as a global financial center. Originally a small agricultural village, Shanghai developed during the late Qing dynasty (1644-1912). Although part of China, the city was controlled by foreign diplomats from various countries, among them were Great Britain, Japan, and France, and you will find many areas within the city, which were built up during these periods of control like the French Concession area. Now let's have a look at the most touristy and magnificent places in Shanghai.

The Bund: The Bund is Shanghai's famous waterfront on the west bank of the River, which separates the city into two parts, Pudong and Puxi.

The charm of Shanghai as a bustling metropolis combining the century-old history and flourishing future is fully presented and is a must-see tourist attraction.

Nanjing Road: China's premier shopping street, the 5.5-kmlong (3.4-mile-long) Nanjing Road, starts at the Bund in the east and ends in the west at the junction of Jing'an Temple and West Yan'an Street, near People Square.

Yu Yuan Garden: Yu Yuan Garden is a classical garden ranking among the must-see attractions in Shanghai. It dates back to the Ming Dynasty (1368-1644) and was owned by a government officer named Pan Yunduan. Yu in Chinese means pleasing and satisfying, and this garden was specially built for Pan's parents as a place for them to enjoy a tranquil and happy time in their old age.

People Square: it's a large square south of Nanjing and north of Huaihai Road. People Square is a spectacular space in the heart of the city. It is a garden-type open space surrounded by buildings and facilities for cultural activities and yes, there is a Tim Hortons for coffee lovers from Canada!!

French Concession also known as Xintiandi: The french concession was a foreign concession from 1849 until 1943. For much of the 20th century, the area covered by the former French Concession remained the premier residential and retail district of Shanghai. Despite re-development over the last few decades, the area retains a distinct character and is a popular tourist destination.

Sasha's on Hengshan Rd and Dongping Rd.: This beautiful villa was once home to Chiang Kai Shek and his wife, Soong Mei Ling. During the civil war, it was taken over by Mao Ze Dong's wife, Jiang Qin. The three-story villa got restored and became the home of Sasha's Fine Dining. It is within walking distance of the building of the First National Congress of the Communist Party of China situated at No.76 Xingye Road, which is next to Xintiandi, a fashionable pedestrian area; the two-story Shikumen building was completed in 1920 and on July 23, 1921, thirteen members held their first national congress of the Communist Party of China here, marking the birth of the Party.

Zapata Bar: Next to Sasha's was a touristy Mexican Tequila bar that also offered great Mexican cuisine in the upstairs dining room.

International Dining/Drinking Spots: There are hundreds of great restaurants and bars in Shanghai, and they will serve and cater to each and every taste and atmosphere you desire, like Paulaner, a German Bier house, which is a popular and successful German restaurant chain in Shanghai and boasts multiple outlets on both sides of the Huangpu. It has one of the best Oktoberfest celebrations outside Munich. You also find many Irish Pubs, French Bistros, and of course, any kind of specialty food representing every part of the world.

Pudong

Pudong is a district of Shanghai located east of Huangpu, the river which flows through central Shanghai. In 1993, the Chinese government set up a Special Economic Zone, creating the Pudong New Area. The western tip of the Pudong district was designated as the Lujiazui Finance and Trade Zone and has become a financial hub of modern China. There are numerous high-rise towers, such as:

Shanghai Tower: 127 Floors, 632 Meters, with an Observation Deck on the 118 Floor, which makes it the world's highest indoor observation deck at 546 Meters.

Oriental Pearl Tower: At 468 Meters, it represents twin Dragons playing with Pearls and architectural and photographic jewel that excites the imagination and attracts thousands of visitors year-round.

Jin Mao Tower: This tower is 420 Meters tall and has an observation area at the 88th Floor at 340 Meters and an excellent Restaurant on the 87th Floor. This is a great place to entertain business associates or just relax with a beautiful view surrounded by many high-rise towers.

Shanghai World Financial Center SWFC: The SWFC is also called the bottle opener based on its shape. At 492 meters, it's the second tallest building in Shanghai. The observation Deck is at 474 Meters. The 2 Floors below and above the opening, Floor 94F at 423 meters, and Floor 97F at 439 Meters are great observation areas to enjoy the view of the Bund and Shanghai.

Shanghai is one of the world's largest seaports and a major industrial and commercial center of China. The city is located on the coast of the East China Sea between the mouth of the Yangtze River (Chang Jiang) to the north and the bay of Hangzhou to the south.

As the saying goes: **You have to see it to believe it.**

UNIQUE EXPERIENCES AND OBSERVATIONS OVER MY MANY JOURNEYS TO CHINA

A water well with fish in it proves that the water is clean and safe

In 2005, I traveled for the first time to China, and over the next few years, I encountered many interesting situations. When I tell these stories to my friends, they seem to enjoy my strange and mostly awkward encounters with many different people and situations in China. As I mentioned earlier, I do not speak Mandarin. I always traveled alone and had to rely on business associates as my contacts, but in the beginning, I did spend most of my time by myself. I was confronted with many interesting incidents and my observations will give you the feeling of having been there with me. You might remember similar encounters in your own life where you did things without really knowing what was going on.

Here are some of my most memorable stories:

Beijing airport:

Returning from Xiamen to Canada was either via Hong Kong, Shanghai, or Beijing. I decided to fly once via Beijing and I took a plane from Xiamen to Beijing. I arrived early in the morning. My flight to Canada was scheduled for after 7 PM, which meant I had over 8 hours and I decided to visit Tiananmen Square and the Forbidden City. I put all my luggage into a locker and went outside to the taxi stands. A friendly taxi controller asked me where I wanted to go and he talked to the taxi driver and told him my destinatio. He told me it would cost 200 RMB and I was on the way. I visited Tiananmen Square and took a lot of pictures and then walked over to the Forbidden City and visited many different areas. I was fascinated by the historical past of the empires. Eventually, I had to return to the airport and I was looking for a taxi stand. I realized that I simply had to flag down a taxi driver. Now the problem was that I had no way of telling the driver where I wanted to go, but luckily I had a brochure from the airport, so I showed him the plane, and he nodded. We went on our way. Arriving at the airport, he showed me the taxi meter and it was at 192 RMB. I gave him 200 RMB. He wanted to return the change, but I told him to keep it as a tip. I walked over to the entrance of the airport, and all of a sudden, a woman came up to me and said that she was with the police. She showed me her badge, and 2 armed policemen were standing behind her.

She asked me where I came from. I told her that I was visiting Tiananmen Square and the Forbidden City. At this point, my heartbeat must have doubled as I knew that Tiananmen Square had a negative political history. Now she wanted to know, how I had got there and I told her that I had come by taxi. She wanted to know how much the fare was. I told her that the meter said 192 RMB but I gave the driver 200 RMB and told him to keep the difference as a tip. She asked me if the driver tried to give me the change and I said yes. She mentioned that tips in China are not legal, but she would accept my explanation. She went on her phone and looked over to the taxi and I noticed that the taxi driver was held by 2 policemen. They answered the phone and then let the driver go. I apologized to the police lady, and she mentioned that they simply try to protect tourists from being ripped off by taxi drivers. I was relieved and went on my way, and slowly my heartbeat went back to normal.

Maglev Speed Train from Pudong Airport to Shanghai Longyang Road.

Maglev was, at that time, the fastest commercial electromagnetic train in the world and had a cruising speed of 431 km/h (268 mph). I arrived from a direct flight from Toronto and after 14 hours, I was a little tired, but I had a lot of time to go to my hotel in Shanghai. Usually, I would get into a taxi, but someone told me about this Maglev Speed Train which uses a non-contact electromagnetic system that makes the train float over a guideway path. After I picked up my luggage, I started walking towards the area where the Maglev sign was directing me. I was able to purchase a ticket for 50 yuan and I walked towards the train. I entered the train and not 10 seconds after I was inside, the train started moving. I was in Europe on many trains and having luggage, it was important to find a storage rack quickly, but I noticed that the train was accelerating; the speed reader showed quickly 431 km/h. I stood there with my luggage, but there was no rattling or jerking like I was used to. I found a seat and held the luggage in front of me and looking outside, it was incredible to see the scenery passing by. We arrived at the destination in less than 8 minutes, and the distance covered was about 30 km.

Taxi in Xiamen:

While working in Xiamen, I got used to taking taxis, and I made sure I always had my destination as well as my hotel on a piece of paper with Chinese writing on it. One day, I was traveling from the hotel to Tongan and there was a lot of traffic. My taxi driver started yelling and gesturing toward another taxi driver and we got stuck in a slow-moving line. The other driver cut in front of us and somehow, the traffic came to a standstill. My taxi driver got out of the car and walked towards the taxi in front of us. He started yelling at the driver, who also exited his car. They started a physical boxing match, hitting each other. Many drivers from the cars ahead and behind us came out to watch, and it looked like they enjoyed this interaction. After a while, a police car was coming from the other direction. The 2 stopped fighting and went back into their taxis, and slowly the traffic started moving again. I told this story to my contact, and again, he laughed and said that this was nothing unusual. Luckily, no police had to get involved.

People Plaza Dance Rituals

In just about every city center in China is a plaza or town square which can be used for dancing rituals. Mostly in the early evenings, people (mostly elderly) gather and dance to rhythmic Chinese music. This practice has its roots in ancient Chinese history, where dancing was part of the exercise and in today's times, dances are performed to mostly Chinese popular songs, both contemporary and historic. It is fascinating to observe the people and the happy faces, smiling and looking very peaceful. One other interesting observation I discovered, was that some of the town squares also host at the side of the square a "marriage" market where parents try to find a partner for their unmarried daughter or son. Typically, the parents or grandparents post sheets of paper detailing the qualities a prospective son- or daughter-in-law should have. It spells out what is expected, and the elderly parents haggle with each other and make it quite clear of their demands. The largest such market is in Shanghai's People Square and I was told there are mostly people from the interior of China where it is difficult to find a suitable partner who could provide for their families, as it is custom that the younger generation will look after the elderly family members.

Tourists in Beijing at the Summer Palace and Imperial Gardens

The Summer Palace in Beijing is a beautiful palace, built halfway up a hill surrounded by lakes and gardens dating back to the Qing dynasty. As I had spent most of my early time in China in Xiamen and Shanghai, I decided on my way home to spend a few days in Beijing to experience some of the touristy areas and ended up at the Summer Palace. It was 35 degrees Celsius, and the sun was smiling. I walked up the many stairs to the palace and after a few hours went back to the bus area. I wanted to buy some postcards and many people were trying to sell me souvenirs, but I just wanted a few postcards. I saw an elderly lady with a sign showing the price for 10 postcards. I liked the idea of not being ripped off and went towards her and bought 10 cards. As soon as I left her, I got approached by another vendor who offered me the same postcards for half price. I told him that this sounds good and I told him that I will buy 10 cards from him, but as soon I said that he disappeared as he was not willing to sell me the cards for half price. He simply wanted to really make the elderly lady look bad. Now in this heat, I was thirsty and saw on the other side of the plaza a young man with a shopping cart box advertising ice-cold drinks. I happily stood in the line-up. In front of me were 2 young American girls. When they got their drinks, they asked how much it costs. The salesman looked at them both and said 30 yuan each and they paid and left. Now I was in China already a few times and knew the cost of basic goods. I asked for an Ice tea, but did not ask for the cost. I gave him 5 yuan and he said thank you. I told this story to my Xiamen contact and he mentioned that the cost should have been a maximum of 3 yuan, so the salesman still made a good profit.

Shopping

In general, shopping at a mall or any regular store is no different than in New York or Paris. Prices are marked and there is no haggling. Of course, you will find many bargains and specials. Sizes you will have to get used to, as an L for me had to be an XXL. There are a lot of well-known stores and in Shanghai, for example, the shopping malls do not differ much from what we are used to. When you're in the food court area, you will feel at home. Line-ups at Starbucks look familiar and if you want a pizza or hamburger, you will have no problem finding what your heart desires. But of course, you will also find many smaller specialty stores in touristy areas like The Bund, Nanjing Road, Yu Yuan Garden, and Xintiandi in Shanghai and each city seems to have its own "Shopping Street."

Open Markets and Hustlers

Antique Flea Market

If you ever visited a flea market in your area, just imagine what it would feel like if it would be 2-3 times the size. I have visited many markets in Europe, Mexico, and North America, but the markets in Beijing, Shanghai, and Xiamen are amazing in size and the variety of goods they sell. This is now the place where the bargaining is in full swing. Tourists are offered bargains of up to 50% off, but when I told my contact how much I paid for a pearl bracelet, he laughed and showed me how it's done. We went back to the same sales stall, and he asked how much they want for a pearl bracelet. He was told the cost is 1500 yuan, but today it can be had for 750 yuan. My contact who is living in China for over 10 years, told him he will pay just 150 yuan, the salesman said no way and we simply walked away. The salesman ran after us and offered 500 yuan and my contact counter offered 250 yuan or 2 bracelets for 500. OK, the salesman said, 2 for 500 is ok and we bought them. One thing you must know in bargaining in China- if you make an offer and it gets accepted, there is no turning back, as they consider your offer like a contract and they may call the police if you refuse to pay. I also discovered an interesting Chinese app that can easily be installed on your phone. You simply take a picture of what you want to buy and they will tell you how much you can buy this same item delivered to you within 1 day. This gives you at least some idea if the price you're paying was worth it or if you would have been better off ordering it online.

Besides all the market stalls and tables, many hustlers are trying to sell you watches, rings, and other trinkets. They usually carry a little box or knapsack, and are quite a nuisance as they will follow you. If you stop and look at their goods, you will be swarmed by every hustler on the market who will tell you that their goods are the best bargain. Unfortunately, a lot of their goods are malfunctioning, (Watches, Cell phones, Laptops, Notebooks, Electronic Games) and you may not know until you actually want to use them or when you're back at your hotel and then it's too late to do anything about it. Always remember the saying: If it's too good to be true, it probably isn't true.

Hotels/Bars/Karaoke

Most Westerners stay in 4 or 5-star hotels, and the service is usually very friendly and the food and drinking areas are pleasant. The hotel restaurants provide you with Englishsubtitled menus and it is very easy for you to have a comfortable meal by yourself. The bar area is usually very quiet. You also can order snacks. Most places offer free WiFi and you can sit with your laptop and look after a business or correspond with your friends at home. Most hotels also have an adjoining Karaoke bar, and if you meet up with friends or business associates it is more than likely that you will be invited to a Karaoke room. There is usually an entrance fee, which will cover your drinks, but most likely whoever invites you will look after this detail. Even if singing is not your forte, remember, everyone is expected to participate. Hopefully, you will find a song to your liking.

Dinner invitations

When you're at a Karaoke room, there will be a lot of people there, mostly friends of your contact, and ever so often you will be approached by one of them. They will ask you where you're from and how long you will be in the area. Your contact, most likely, had told them about you and they might invite you to attend a dinner that they are hosting in the next few days. They will tell you quite frankly that they would want you at the dinner and there is nothing you need to do other than be there. They will offer to have a translator present during the dinner as there will be mostly just Chinese-speaking people. He tells you that it will be very advantageous for him to introduce a Westerner, which will show his associate that he has international connections. Over the years, I attended many such dinners and was able to make several new connections.

Attending a Wedding

One morning while at breakfast, my Shanghai contact came unexpectedly and asked if I could attend a wedding that evening. He said a school friend of his is getting married and the groom would like to show the family of his bride that he has international connections. My contact said he will be there with me and there is nothing I need to do other than be there. My Shanghai contact was the person who grew up at the French Concession in Shanghai. He had shown me many intriguing areas of Shanghai and I agreed to attend. Luckily, I had a suit with me on that trip and went to the location of the wedding. I arrived, and my contact introduced me to the groom and the wedding party before it was time to take the seats. To my biggest surprise, I was seated at the head table and my contact was seated way back in the room. He came over and said, just observe and smile a lot.

Dinner was very nice. After cutting the wedding cake there were speeches by various guests. All of a sudden, my contact came over and told me that it is my turn to talk now. He said just say some greetings and how happy you are to have been invited by the groom to attend this wedding and he will translate. He handed me the microphone and needless to say, it was an unusual moment for me to talk. I have no idea what he translated into Chinese, but everyone seemed happy and applauded. This is China, and this was one of the most unusual experiences for me.

Food and the shake test

Chinese Food sounds good to Westerners, but for Chinese, there is no general meaning to Chinese Food. Each region and city have its speciality. We may know Szechuan and Hunan Food, but in Shanghai, it's Shanghainese food while in Xiamen or Yancheng or Beijing, only their area food counts. The best advice is to let the person you're with order whatever they consider as appropriate. If you're with someone from Anhui, he will find a restaurant that serves Anhui food and the same goes for every region's speciality. Chinese people are very proud of their food heritage, and they feel very happy if they see that you enjoy their food. As I am sometimes a little picky about what I like, I use the allergy excuse to get out of certain food types. At one point a business partner of mine ordered steamed shrimps, the dish was covered and when they took the lid off, the dish was full of steam and the shrimps were still moving he told me that this is a delicatessen, which has to be enjoyed as long the shrimps are still alive and he eats one after the other and the shrimp tails were still moving when he put it in his mouth.

Needless to say, I did not eat the shrimps and from that day on, when I had lunch or dinner with my business associate, I would tell him that he can order anything he wants, as long he lets me do a shake test before I eat. Shake Test? he asked. Yes, I told him I will get the food on my plate and then I will shake the plate and then put it down and look at the food and if it keeps moving, I will not eat it. I think at first, he was a little irritated by my remark, but after that, he always offered me to do the shake test. He thought it was funny, and I know he told this story to all his friends. I still use this phrase sometimes, but only with people who know me well and who know that I don't mean to put down any kind of Chinese food.

Portuguese Custard Tarts

One day, my Shanghai contact showed me around the old areas of Shanghai where he grew up, including the school he attended. We walked toward a plaza, and on a side street I noticed a lot of people lined up in front of a bakery. He quickly lined up as well and told me that these were the best and original custard tarts you can find anywhere. After about 20 minutes, we were at the front of the line, and got 6 tarts. I immediately ate one. They were still hot as they had just come out of the oven. I complimented them, and said they tasted incredible. I told him we have similar custard tarts in Canada in Portuguese bakeries. **He got a little irritated and told me that these custard tarts originated in China and then Marco Polo came to China and stole the recipe and brought it back to Portugal.** Wow, I just got a history lesson, but I do love these custard tarts.

Buddhist Monastery

I was traveling by car with my Shanghainese contact from

Shanghai to Hangzhou and halfway, he told me that there is a Buddhist Monastery up in the mountain region. He asked me if it would be ok with me to go visit his friend who lives in the Monastery. Of course, I had no objection. We ascended about halfway up the hill, where we had to park the car and walk up the hill to the temple. We were greeted by his friend and they performed a ceremony around an open fire pit. It was interesting to watch as they interacted in prayer and singing.

After that, we were invited to have dinner at the monastery with all the other people living there. I was told that there was no meat and it was ok with me, but all of a sudden, one man came to the table and told us that they have chicken in the kitchen and they can prepare me a special meal. I accepted and enjoyed the atmosphere. I was told that it was very unusual to have a Westerner attending their dinner. Again, this episode gave me some insights into China I never knew about.

There are many more little incidents and stories I could talk about, but I hope you get the picture of what I'm trying to convey about my Chinese experiences.

In the second part of my writing, I will mostly talk about my experiences doing business in China. You will find out how I had to learn the ropes in helping to set up manufacturing locations. The way I learned to succeed is by learning from my many mistakes in the beginning. Even so, it will tell stories mostly about business. There are many areas which will be of interest to you, and you will see how business in China is conducted as well as the interactions between the government agencies, bankers, and lawyers. Most importantly, you will also learn about the intensity of the average Chinese worker and the pride they put forward in their work.

It will offer you a new way to look at goods **MADE IN CHINA.**

Part 2

A Guide How To Navigate Through The Business Jungle In China As A "White Man"

A Guide How To Navigate Through The Business Jungle In China

As A "White Man"

Introduction to my China Business Adventures
When in China, do as the Chinese do!
Reasons to expand your business into China
My Lessons learned during my 50+ business trips to China

General and Basic Business Principals for Success in China

-Activity Based Costing-Chinese Lawyer-TranslatorGovernment regulations-

-Labour Relations-Management Team-Banking-Financial Statements-China Audit

Conclusions of My Lessons Learned in China and now ask yourself one more time:

Why would you set up your manufacturing business in China?

INTRODUCTION TO MY CHINA BUSINESS ADVENTURES

Mainland Chinese are very simple in classifying people:

You are either Chinese or Asian or Black or White and there is no in-between

They do not care much about where you come from. Being an American, European, or Australian is about as detailed as they will classify you and assume that if you are white, you must have a lot of money.

White people are called "Big Nose" or "Long Nose" and you will hear them calling you "Laowai," which means either foreigner or outsider. I know of some Westerners who are upset when they hear this. However, in general, White people are treated with a sense of quiet acceptance, as most Chinese understand that the reason the White people are there is to either bring tourist money or investment money and create jobs. Chinese people understand that their factories are busy because they produce goods for White people.

But why would you want to do business in China?

What makes you think that China is the answer to your current state of business? Is it because you read or know of competitors who are outsourcing their production to China and lowering their costs and offering lower pricing? Does the lure of producing your goods in this low-cost country really make sense to you? Do you have the capacity and structure in your business to even consider a move to China?

Questions galore with no fixed answers. You can ask 100 people who did or do business with China over the last 10 years and you will get 100 different answers to your question and many more opinions about "should have and could have." There is no manual or guidebook that shows you what path to follow. Yes, many experts are talking about China, but their advice is all expressed in generalizations and most of the time it might not be applicable to your situation, or the cost of following their advice is way over your ability to proceed.

Do I have the answers for you?

No, I do not claim to have all your answers as each venture is different. What I have is a wealth of real-life experiences you can build on. I will tell you some stories of Aliens in China (Alien is the word they use for us on the immigration card). You will read real-life stories of Westerners who have tried and gave up...tried and succeeded...tried and failed.

Learn from my mistakes and draw from my experiences on what to do or what not to do when doing business in mainland China, I will give you a "Western" look at the ins and outs of China and how to avoid the pitfalls of not knowing the "Chinese Way" of doing business.

I will tell you stories of businesspeople who are very successful in their own country, who come to China and have to go through the "Kindergarten" stage of China. There is nothing that can prepare you for the situations you might stumble upon, and no guidebook or China report can tell you about the many awkward and curious situations you may encounter.

And yes, **China is a strong authoritarian country with a mountain of red tape** for any situation. However, the new China is also very entrepreneurial and sometimes more capitalistic than any Western country, which means money is not the only factor to get things going your way.

From my experiences and the experiences of my business friends, you can gain a valuable understanding of my writing about life in China. When you read **The White Man's China**, you will be able to draw your own conclusions and use or discard anything you read. I will be happy to receive your comments. Send me an email and I will discuss any questions and concerns in private or public through this medium.

Just always keep in mind that **whatever you know about China today will be obsolete by tomorrow.** This is the advice I received from the Mayor of Xiamen after signing a land agreement in 2005. His advice has guided me throughout my business ventures over the years. **Never take anything for granted, as the situation can change with no warning or reason from one day to the other in the wink of your eye.**

WHEN IN CHINA, DO AS THE CHINESE DO!

Always be mindful that you do not get a second chance to make a good first impression. Build trust by immersing yourself in Chinese cultural practices and learning to respect and understand the various ancient rituals and following some basic Chinese business etiquette. Many situations might produce some awkward moments, but simply relax and be aware of some of the simple ways you can show your appreciation for your Chinese friend's way of life.

Basic Chinese Business Etiquette

Greetings: Wait for the Chinese counterpart to offer their hand first for a "Western-style" handshake. Hand out your business card with both hands with the legible side facing the recipient so they can read it. **After you receive their business card in return, examine the business card, and never put it in your shirt pocket or trousers as it would suggest a lack of respect. The card should be placed visibly during the meeting**.

Business Meals and Seating arrangements: If the dinner is in a separate room around a round table, the principal attendee and Guest sit together the furthest away from the door.

Food: Arranging the food should be left to the Chinese partner or have your translator order the food way in advance. Traditionally, every dish will be presented to you first and politely help yourself with every dish. Never empty your plate as an empty plate indicates that there was not enough food to your liking. I also made it a habit to tell my partner in advance which foods I was allergic to.

Maotai/Toasts: It is customary to have a toast before the meal. Each member on your table who is a supervisor or higher will come over and offer a toast and in return. It is expected that you will visit each one later and offer a toast to them as well. Moatai is a fairly high grade toast. You have to be careful not to get too overwhelmed with drinking, but with the main people on your table, you definitely have to do "Gangbei," which means "empty cup." It is expected that you empty your shot glass.

Gift exchanges: The best way to offer a gift is to have your translator mention it first to the person whom you have a gift for and find out if a presentation at the table or after the meal in the parking lot is more appropriate. If you offer a gift to a person on the table, you might get some anguish or jealous looks from some people.

Networking-Karaoke: After a nice meal it is often customary that you will be invited to join the party at a Karaoke room and have an enjoyable evening. Don't be shy and participate with at least one song. You will be amazed how the Chinese people love to sing, and don't forget to applaud after every song. Some places also offer card or dice games. So, the more you participate, the more trust you build up within your group.

Colors: Red and more red is the most beloved color in China **Numbers: anything with an 8 will be lucky**, but stay away from 4 or 14

Dragon: The Dragon will always be the favorite symbol in China

The art of communication: Any talk about traditional

Chinese festivals is a great starting point. Show interest in the achievements of their ancestors and listen to their stories. Talk about similarities of your Western culture to the Chinese culture.

Chinese Festivals: Spring Festival (known as the Chinese New Year)

Lantern Festival: Qing Ming Festival: Duan Wu Festival: Qi Xi Festival:

Mid-Autumn Festival: Chong Yang Festival:

Always have a Chinese calendar by your side, and mark all festivals. The Chinese are always surprised, but very happy if you mention their festivals. They love telling you stories about the origins of their special festivals.

Business Negotiations:

I just about forgot to mention that business is no topic at any dinner. Most likely, you had left the business meeting at their offices without a clear decision about your issues, which needed to be looked after. **When it is time to say good night, simply ask the main partner when you can expect an answer about the meeting issues** and if he is a government official, **he most likely will tell you that he will have to call Beijing now and he will tell you the answer in the morning. If this is the case, you know that you will get your way because your issues are most likely not at a level of Beijing.** He just said that to his employees, who were present, think that the decisions are all made in Beijing.

Always remember that communication is the key and understanding the cultural differences within China is more important than what any China expert can tell you. What works in Shanghai may not work in Beijing and certainly will be totally different in Jilin or Xiamen or Shenzhen, and when I say works, I mean the way you approach a business start-up and your negotiations with local government officials. Each area of China has its own characteristics. You need to get a feel for each area and adapt your thinking accordingly.

"Made in China" seems to be the most common phrase, but if you want to do business in China, think of "Made for China."

REASONS TO EXPAND INTERNATIONALLY AND WHY CONSIDER CHINA?

Always be certain of what you want to achieve and depending on your business, may it be in Trade or Manufacturing, always consider the following issues:

Trade Business:

What products do you want to buy/sell? How many "middlemen" will be involved? Can you buy direct from the manufacturer?

Consider the advantages of being a local customer or supplier as some customers will not trust your products since they are "Made in China," unless your pricing is at such a low level that nothing else matters.

Manufacturing Business:

The cost advantage of foreign production labor. Volume must be justified to open overseas production. Also always consider the possibility of your production sales in the China market and other countries.

What form of a foreign manufacturing plant?

Each of the following methods has advantages and disadvantages

Wholly owned business: Wholly owned business gives you 100% control, but as a foreigner, you might experience extra costs and time delays to get production and export permits, and various dealings with governmental agencies. **Another consideration is the money flow between your companies.** This could be an issue as **foreign money transactions are tightly guarded and supervised by the Chinese Foreign Exchange agency.**

Joint Venture: a JV (Joint Venture) is an easier way to get started as your Chinese Partner will know how to speed up approvals and get around other regulations. However, you might find that there is interference from your JV Partner, and possibly sabotage of your know-how (stealing of intellectual property/patents) could be a big problem in the future. Your partner will also quickly suggest that you hire some friends of his and even if they are highly qualified, be very careful to let them take control of your business. **Remember that most likely, you personally will be in China just on certain occasions, and unless you have trusted personnel, you could easily lose control.**

Sub-Contractor: Sub-Contract can be financially the easiest way, but you will always have to rely on someone else to live up to their agreements, and it becomes very difficult when sub-standard parts are being produced and shipped (who pays for what). **Dealing directly with a sub-contractor is a safe way to keep control of your business.** It is better than if you buy through an agency as they will markup your products, but they will not take any responsibility for the products, and quality issues are difficult to reconcile.

MY LESSONS LEARNED DURING MY 50+ BUSINESS TRIPS TO CHINA

Chapter 1 The Business "Tourist"

I have been to China….I know China….I hear these words many times and when I ask a few questions, I quickly realize that I am talking to a "tourist" even if he pretends to be a "business" man. Visiting China and actually doing business in China are two different things. **A "tourist" will be guided to see the beauties of China** and be guarded against the true picture of mainland China. **The same applies to a visiting "business" man who is purchasing goods from China.** He will be protected to see just what the Chinese supplier wants him to see. Most of the time, he will be chauffeured around to all the touristy places. He will stay in a 5-star hotel, eat Westernstyle breakfast, and get treated to first-class Chinese restaurants for dinner. The "business" part of the trip will be spent in elaborate offices, and he will attend the obligatory tea ceremony in the boss's office. Then, they walk you through the production and quality control area and all looks very impressive the first time you see this. The working people wear nice uniforms and smile when a visitor walks around the plant. They all look so happy and content but don't believe for a minute that this is not all staged for the visitor who comes here to spend his money. Of course, the largest obstacle is the language. Very few people will speak English and the ones who do are difficult to understand. If the company does much business with the West, then they have 1 or 2 employees who speak English, but most people hire a temporary interpreter, who has no idea about the business and any question you ask will be translated and answered in a manner that makes it clear that the interpreter had no idea what your question was.

Just because a Chinese answers your questions with a positive yes, yes, yes… it does not mean that he even understood your question. A Chinese will not admit that he did not understand as this would show weakness, and he does not want to lose his face (an expression which is a reality, but not understood very well by Westerners and shunned by the Chinese as they will never admit to such a thing).

Depending on the importance of the visitor, he will get the best treatment based on his contribution to the business and the prospect of future and additional business. **All such "business" visits are carefully staged** and well-designed to keep the visitor happy. Don't be fooled by pricing alone. You may be able to save much money by purchasing goods from China, but you may not get the benefit of the "true" savings which your competitor may get if they are willing to tackle their China business on a direct basis and not through wellconnected middlemen and jobbers which use Alibaba to attract customers. You pay a heavy price penalty and there is no quality guarantee as you are not in control of how the products are contracted. What you see may not be what you get.

I had many discussions with businesspeople who have used China suppliers. They complain about reliability and quality. I always ask the same question: how much are your savings compared to if you produce or purchase locally? If the answer is more than 60%, I always suggest that they renegotiate at a slightly higher price, but with stringent conditions on material usage and quality inspections. I had an owner of a tooling shop purchase multi-cavity tooling molds for plastic parts. The best local quote he received was $40,000 and his calculation for producing this mold in-house at his shop was around $30,000. He received a China quote for $12,000 based on his drawings. He told me that he appreciated the savings, but when the tools got here, he had to spend a lot of time adjusting, and the tools needed maintenance on a much more frequent basis than the local tools. I suggested he ask the China supplier to quote based on your tool material specifications using Japanese steel instead of Chinese steel. The quote came in at $15,000, which still was a 50% savings, but required very little extra cost for maintenance compared to local material. I met the tool shop owner the other day, and he told me that most of his problems with the China supplier were solved and only when he gets greedy and goes for the lowest price does he get burned as human nature will always occasionally go for the quick buck and overrule common sense.

In my next chapter, I will give you some insights into the costs of doing business directly and what you must watch for to get a fair shake in your China dealings.

Chapter 2 You May Think That Everything In China Is Cheap!

A major misconception is the assumption that everything in China is cheap. It really depends on your taste and willingness to adapt, but most foreigners will want some familiarity with what they expect to get. This applies food to clothing, accessories, electronics, and other personal items. No matter if you are a tourist or a seasoned traveler, you will run into this problem over and over again. In major cities like Shanghai or Beijing, you find English-speaking sales personnel in hotels and large department stores, and in these types of places, there are set pricing policies and bargaining is frowned upon. All the brand names of clothing, watches, handbags, etc., are priced at levels well above Paris, London, or New York and **the stores are filled with Chinese people lining up to get the latest Gucci or LV bag at prices well above a regular worker's monthly income**. However, when you wander around on the main shopping street, **you will encounter many people who will tell you about the "bargain" stores**. There are at least 3 levels of these "stores" which are based on quality and price, depending on your taste and willingness to accept lesser-quality goods. You can find great bargains from scarves, ties, shirts, wallets, bags, shoes, and all kinds of electronic equipment. When you accept to visit such a location, you will be guided into alleyways and enter a building with long hallways, and steep stairways and eventually you find the "special room."

As all these places are illegal, you cannot expect a refund policy in place, but there are also many small legit stores around, where you can bargain for discounts as most items do not have a price tag. **As a tourist, they will quote you a price well above its value and as a novice bargainer, you may think that you got a great deal with the 25% discount which you negotiated**. Unless you are in a hurry and really want this particular trinket, never mention a price, as they may accept, and you can then not change your mind. They consider the price you mentioned as a contract and will hold you to it. It is not worth getting involved with the authorities over this and you will lose most of the time. Offer a maximum of 25% of its original price they mentioned and then let it ride and see how low it will go. Start walking away and if your offer was reasonable, you will get to buy it at your price or at least close to it.

Now that you have the shopping part behind you and feel that you made great strides in understanding how the Chinese economy work, **you are now ready to tackle the real reason why you are in China... Business!**

No matter what kind of business you are in, you will need to connect with local manufacturers and suppliers of the goods you are looking for. Unless you already have some connections, some agencies will arrange meetings for you and drive you around and even provide an interpreter for the day. Try to visit about 3 suppliers who offer similar capabilities a day, and explain to them what you are looking for and listen to their proposals. They will show you their quality room filled with samples of past and current production. **Ask for a quick ballpark pricing on some of the items you see and you will notice quickly how competitive they are. Most will refuse to quote any pricing, and this should raise red flags for you.** They like to play the same game with you like the store owner who just dropped his price to 25% of his original quote. **Never give away what price you would accept. Let them give you the best price possible, and then tell them that you are on your way to visit the next supplier**.

I assume you know your business and you understand the manufacturing process as well as the competitive pricing in your country. If the process is heavily labor-oriented, keep the following in mind: Shanghai minimum wages for 2016 were around 2220 RMB, which is about USD 341 for 160 hours which translates fully costed including social benefits to about USD 2.80 per hour. Now compare this to your own cost structure in your factory, and you can estimate what pricing should be forthcoming. Also keep in mind that Shanghai has the highest minimum wages and highest social costs in China. **Some provinces in the interior like Hubei, Henan, or anywhere north of the Yangzi River will have minimum wages at close to half to the Shanghai wages**. There will be extra costs for transportation to the seaport. However, depending on volumes, this difference can be insignificant to the overall costs.

In my next chapter, I will talk about the different manufacturing locations and the pros and cons you need to consider.

Chapter 3 Where To Produce Is The Big Question!

Let us assume that you are a businessman, either an owner or a top manager. You know your business inside out and **you hear that your competitors are outsourcing their production to China.** Your margins are getting squeezed and your customers are comparing your pricing against your competitors. Your latest RFQ for a replacement job was returned for a requote. Your customer likes your quality rating of 0 PPM and he wants to give you a second chance at the business, but **he tells you that your labor and overhead rates were not comparable to your competitor quotes**. This job represents about 20 percent of your business and if you lose this work, you might have to lay off 15 staff and your remaining jobs will become less profitable due to the increased overheads.

If at this point you do not have an **Activity Based Costing System**, you should take immediate steps to implement this and then you can make an educated decision about your future. **Based on the true cost of your production, it will help you to justify your next move.** This also is the time when you need to adjust your current and future business plans, as it is important to keep your local banker or financial partner informed. **You have a few options: stay the course and reduce the business volume, outsource some of your production, or produce certain parts of your business in a low-cost country**. Either way, you may need financial support to act upon your chosen path. If you decide to do nothing and let the business reductions take effect, waiting and hoping that the business climate eventually changes, the viability of your business may be questioned by your banker or financial partner.

Based on your ABC costing breakdown, you may be able to justify an investment into an expansion project in China. Requote your replacement job to your customer and base it on China costs. Ask your customer permission to ship Chinese-produced parts that are totally under your control. **If the price is right, based on your past quality record, you may get this job awarded to you and you can start your "China" venture.**

Now, where do you start? First, check out where your competitors are producing or outsourcing their parts. If this information is not easily available, ask your suppliers if they also supply your competitors and they will tell you stories of how they were forced to switch their supply base once they outsourced or directly moved the production to China. **Your suppliers probably know exactly what is going on in your industry and who is competitive in your field.**

Next, **you must decide what kind of China setup you want.** There are many different forms of companies you can establish, and I suggest you consider one of the following 3 options:

-A Contractual Joint Venture (JV) with a local Chinese manufacturer

-An Equity Joint Venture (EJV) with a local Chinese company

-A Wholly Foreign Owned Enterprise (WFOE).

Then look around for an appropriate location. Most people start looking around the Shanghai area, which has the biggest and most experienced labor pool, but also the highest minimum wage scale. Surrounding provinces, such as Jiangsu, Zhejiang, and Jiangxi, or more to the interior like Hubei, Henan, or Northern provinces such as Jilin or Hebei. However, always keep in mind the climate of China. Northern provinces have very long cold winters and transportation may become an issue, interior and more in the Southern provinces like Fujian, Hunan, and Guangdong have summers with temperatures above the mid-30s with very high humidity. In most China factories, air conditioning or heating is unheard of, and workers demand a heating bonus above 35 degrees. In the winter, they wear heavy coats and especially heavy gloves, which may impede the quality of their parts, depending on the difficulty of assembly of your products.

At this stage, you may have to consider now a recon mission to China. Decide on 2 or 3 cities you would want to visit and arrange with an agency to show you around. Visit companies who produce similar products like your company and look around if simply outsourcing or actual product is in your best interest. **Make it clear that you may be looking for a JV partner and you will receive quickly the attention of many Chinese entrepreneurial companies**.

In my next chapter, we look at the political side of issues you encounter once you decide a move your production to China.

Chapter 4 Beware Of Hustlers And Politics

It is said that China is the new Wild West.... check out any old Western movie, where the Gunslinger, the Sheriff, and the Judge are the only ones to control the law in town, and you get to know the meaning of the new China. **The Chinese laws are centrally controlled by very few Party Officials in Beijing. However, most of China is ruled by local independent government officials who interpret the Beijing directives in a variety of ways. Their decisions are far-reaching and binding to the public and very difficult to understand for outsiders.** Power is in the hands of very few and for getting anything accomplished in a reasonable time, **you need to understand the rules of the game**. The local government officials have very little opposition and a great deal of authority. **A clear sign that you will not get your way right away is the use by the officials of the Beijing excuse, and this is a great wall that the officials can hide behind. Of course, there is no Beijing that will get involved in minor decisions,** but it is an indication of other options you may have to pursue and that is where you have to make quick decisions based on personal observations of the issues at hand. Should you feel that you want a more detailed explanation of any decision, you quickly will hear the words **that they will have to check with Beijing or that a "friend" of the government will offer his services**. If you are stuck and really need some answers, this is a quick way to find out what it takes to get things done. The recommended consultant who got referred by the government official will guide you step by step on what you have to do to achieve your goal. The fee you have to pay for his services will be well worth it if he really has the right connections. **Put a deadline for your request with payment after completion and you may get smooth sailing from then on. He will be a good contact to have for other issues where you will need help.**

On the other hand, there will be many people approaching you and they will tell you **stories about how they helped foreigners do business**

in China and how you can take advantage of officials with a little incentive.

I strongly advise you to stay away from these hustlers and never accept such an offer, as they will use this against you and threaten you if you should stop using their "services."

The best way to get things done is to ask the government official if they can recommend a consultant who can help you prepare all the documents you need to submit. They will happily recommend someone, and then you can be assured that you will get the best possible service. **Know exactly what you want to achieve and be specific about the timeframe required**. There will always be hints about meeting with committee members and an invitation for lunch or dinner would be very suitable for such meetings. Depending on how well you know the area, it probably is a good idea for such a meeting to be held at your hotel. The setting will be in a large room with a round table that can seat up to 20 people and no matter who you invite for this "meeting," each seat will be occupied. You will sit opposite the door and the person you invited will sit right beside you. If this person does not speak English, you will need an interpreter on your left in order to have a conversation during the meal. Leave ordering the food to your guest or your interpreter who will make arrangements with the serving personnel as most places have set menus for such gatherings. Drinks will be either beer or mao-tai, a highpercentage alcohol rice wine. **Cheers are compulsory in China, but on an individual basis, and it's best to understand the meaning of "Ganbei" really quickly and how much "Ganbei" you can absorb as it literally means "empty cup."** Try to offer this to your "important" guests only and when other people come over just do a small sip with them. The percentage of this drink can go as high as 62%, and if the quality is poor, your head will feel it real quickly. Chinese people love to see Westerners getting drunk and they insist that you keep drinking. Of course, they will keep also drinking and keep in mind that their tolerance for alcohol is usually quite low. Said all that, **dinner will always be an experience as you will see dishes that cannot be classified in any category the way we Westerners know Chinese food**. I will talk about food etiquette in more detail in a later chapter.

Once the meal is over, most people will simply leave and only your guest will actually say goodbye to you. **You will not know if it was a successful meeting until the day after when you will get the answer on how you are progressing with your project, but always assume that all went well.**

In my next chapter, we look at the kind of team you need to build around you to succeed and some rookie mistakes to avoid.

Chapter 5 Build A Solid Team And Avoid Costly Rookie Mistakes

Your glowing business plan, which you presented to your banker and financial partner will do little for you if you cannot build a solid team around you. You may be able to convince your financial partner, but words are one thing and actions are another. As the saying goes:

"Actions Speak Louder than Words." It is of utmost importance that you know the capabilities of your current staff and do not overestimate the willingness of your local people to make this venture a success. Expansion and especially expansion in the Far East can be a very intimidating task for your staff and their fear of failure is real and can become a handicap that is hard to overcome for them. **Some will be enthusiastic about the adventure aspect of going to China, but as soon as the novelty wears off and the "real" work begins they will find every excuse in the book to tell you why they cannot continue.**

You need to surround yourself with a few experts, some local and some in China and when I say local, it does not mean that it has to be your current staff. Key at your home plant will be an experienced Plant Manager who understands your business inside out and who is willing to competently train new people. This person must be willing to work onsite at your China location for a few weeks at a time and transfer his knowledge to local Chinese personnel. Since your products are unique, it would be difficult to hire someone in China with these skills.

In China, you will need a local lawyer, who is experienced in dealing with foreign companies, and you will need an **office manager who can overlook the bookkeeping,** purchasing, invoicing, and personnel issues, a **production manager, experienced in machine set-ups** and a basic understanding of tool maintenance, and a **competent TS or ISO certified quality control manager. English knowledge will be a requisite for the lawyer, office manager, production manager, and quality control manager.** Your lawyer should be a local person with good connections to the labor department, the police, and the communist party officials. The lawyer will also arrange an interpreter for you when attending government functions, dinners, and general business meetings with potential suppliers.

Make sure that your company has the image of a Chinese company as the regular employees will demand higher wages if you show off your proud Western heritage too much.

This brings me to the **Rookie mistakes and the hard lesson company of a business associate of mine had to go through**. His story has guided me in my future dealings in China and the lessons learned helped me to avoid similar mistakes. This was a successful privately owned mid-sized company with plants in multiple countries. The owners decided to expand to China to take advantage of the low-cost manufacturing everyone was talking about. Their business plan was presented to their local bank and a budget was approved, which included building a factory and moving partial production to China. The announcement in their head office location was applauded and through a friend of the owner, they contracted an entrepreneur living in China. This was a great way to get started. After visiting China, it was decided to buy land and build a factory. The costs seemed reasonable compared to what such a building would cost in their hometown. Little did they know that the costs were double what a Chinese company would have charged to build such a plant. Yes, the quality may have been better, but it was not worth the extra costs. Being a proud Western company, they started hiring people with English knowledge for most of the office and managerial positions. Even the receptionist was fluent in English. Instead of paying 3-5000 RMB per month, her wages were above 10,000. The same with engineers whereas a Chinese-speaking engineer would get 6-8,000 and with English 15-20,000 and so it went with most positions and overheads went out of control. On top of this, instead of having the support of 1 production manager from their head office, they brought in on average 4 to 5 production workers on a monthly basis to support the new company. The regular workers all saw this and since this was a Western company, they demanded higher wages. Compared to the head office wage calculations, this was still reasonable, but little did they know that the competitors who produced in China were way more competitive and the money they thought they saved with this move was squandered on extravagant procedures which were way out of line for China. Needless to say, the company closed down after 2 years, and never was able to acquire any new business within China.

In my next chapter, we look at the "Chinese Way" of doing business.

Chapter 6 The "Chinese Way" Of Doing Business

I heard the following phrases over and over from my Chinese colleagues......

You have to learn to do Business the "Chinese

Way."

-You don't understand the "Chinese Way."

-this is China and you have to do business the "Chinese Way."

What makes sense to you, unfortunately, does not make sense to a Chinese. I often wondered why our way of doing business is so different from the "Chinese Way." China is a new entrepreneurial country, and the young people are adapting to our way of life, but the older people who grew up under strict communist rule and education are now free to experience what they call the new society with their own rules. **We would maybe call this "special favors" or even corruption, but some Chinese see it more like a cost of doing business. People in power have all the cards and demand respect through these "special favors"** and it is quite normal that your manager will get a contribution from his workers every month for having the privilege to work for him. It is something like a union due and it assures the workers of receiving fair treatment. As a foreigner, we will never know this, as this is all cash under the table money, and nobody will come forward as this seems to be an acceptable practice. The same goes for your suppliers but we will deal with this in my next chapter.

Chinese workers are very good workers, as anyone employing Chinese workers in our Western culture can contest. They are very proud workers and want to do the best job possible for the company. However, in China, some colleagues tell me that productivity is at very low levels compared to their home factories. **Since the wages are very**

low, some Westerners also discount the work expectations, but this is a grave mistake. I was told that a Chinese worker would produce at about 60% of a Western worker, and when we started production, which was a direct transfer from our home production, I observed the workers, and they took their time to produce the same parts which previously were produced in our home factory. I took a video from our home factory with a Vietnamese worker doing the same job. I asked the Chinese workers why a Vietnamese worker in the West could produce 40 to 50 percent more than a worker in China. The answer was a big surprise to me, as they told me that Vietnamese workers must work harder because they come from a poor country and need to work twice as hard as Chinese workers. I asked what it would take to produce here at the same level as in our Western factories and again, the answer was simple; they wanted to know how much bonus they can get if they produce at the same level. My answer was that the bonus is that they still will have a job after the 3-month probation period, and as long as we are competitive and get new jobs they will have work. One older lady worker, who also had a nephew who was working for us, asked for the quota required . She produced at that level the following day and ever since, and so did her nephew, who was just 19 years old. I promised all the workers a bonus of 10 RMB (about $1.60) a day when they produced the given quota with 0 rejections. **It took less than a week, and our overall production was above 100% of our Western factory production**.

When I talk about low wages, other benefits are of importance and expected from the workers. After 4 hours of work, a meal must be provided for all employees. We would cater the food at about 6 RMB (about $1) per meal/employee. Heat bonus of about 10 RMB a day above 35 degrees, transportation to and from work from/to a central town location, as there was no public transit to our factory, and an attendance bonus of 100 RMB per month if no missed days (missed days are deducted from the monthly pay pro-rated) and of course overtime pay for any hour worked over the mandatory 48 hours per week at a time and a half pay. In that way, nothing is expected for free and more dedication to the job lets a worker earn that little extra which makes them happy. A few days before the Chinese New Year there is a company party, and all employees receive a gift and a cash bonus in a red envelope.

As I mentioned earlier, **there are different rules and attitudes in China. What seems not fair in our society is absolutely acceptable in China.** You still can ask any question you want on the application form, such as age, sex, national status (if from a minority or mainstream national) religious trend, question about being a member of the Communist party, and health issues. There are no questions off-limit.

In my next chapter, we talk about Sales the "Chinese Way."

Chapter 7 The "Chinese Way" Of Sales In China

Now you must examine your decision to start up your production in China. What was the final push that made you decide? Was it to transfer your current production to a low-cost country and improve your margins? Was it to stay competitive with your competitors who try to take over your current or replacement business by offering lower costs to your current customers? Did your current customers demand that you sign up for an LTA with givebacks as high as 4-4-4-4? You tell me how you can find 16% savings on your current production over the next 4 years? How does your competitor do it? The answer most likely is the location of the production and this applies to Europe as well as North America. There are certain areas that still can be competitive, but **your customers do not care anymore where the production takes place. They are just interested in the lowest costs possible with acceptable quality standards.**

Now you decided to start up your production in China. **You must be thinking that with a factory in China, you can also start selling your products in the China market.** Looking around, you will find that your current customers also have factories in China, and this should make it easy to get some business for you. Well, this can be, unfortunately, a very misleading way of thinking. **You will find that your current customers and their business unit in China are quite separate and independent from their head office in Europe or North America, and the Chinese management will mostly deal with Chinese suppliers only.**

The fact that you supply to their European or North American business units has no bearing on the decision the Chinese operation will take in regard to your business. I was at a meeting with FAW in Changchun and I was in the understanding that VW Wolfsburg has the final say about any products being purchased for their Audi production. Just after we opened a production facility in Northern China, we arranged a meeting with FAW purchasing in Changchun to introduce our new facility and ask to be put on the RFQ list for any new parts requirements. There were 5 purchasing agents, and all were Chinese, including the head of purchasing. He made it quite clear that purchasing decisions are made by him and not by the head office, as this is a joint venture business. We made a presentation of our products which included some parts we supply to other automotive customers, and his reaction and comment was as follows: **We have 3 very competent Chinese suppliers for the same kind of product already; why should I add you to that list?**

However, there are still some Tier 1 companies that are controlled by their head office in North America and Europe, but even there, you will run into the supply chain of mostly Chinese companies who supply products at a very low price. The only real advantage we could offer is engineering support, which is lacking by some if not most Chinese suppliers.

Now, this was the easy part to contact transplant customers from Europe and North America, **but how about breaking into the Chinese market of all the purely Chinesecontrolled companies?** First, you must find an experienced Chinese sales manager. This is not an easy task, as in every interview, you will hear that they can do anything. **Ideally, the salesperson should have an engineering background and speak English in order for you to make sure he can competently represent your products.** He will want a fairly high base wage and a commission on sales and quickly, he will ask for a budget with special considerations for the potential buyers. **Sales are achieved with relationships and special favors.** This may not be too obvious for foreign transplants, but certainly for purely Chinese companies. It is quite common that a purchasing agent will tell you the percentage commission he receives from your competitors, and he will tell you his expectations if he actually would consider your products. He will provide you with a target price and many salesmen will then offer to split their own commission in half and share it with the purchasing manager in order to get the business awarded.

I realize that we consider such tactics very unethical. However, this is what you are faced with in China. If you don't play along, you will have no chance to acquire a Chinesecontrolled business. The same system is applied with plant approvals, and ISO or TS certifications. They are quite open in discussing how much extra effort they must put forward for you in order for you to get a good rating and how much this effort is worth to your competitors.

Well, this is the "Chinese Way" of doing business in China.

In my next chapter, we will talk about the Chinese Way of purchasing and developing a supply base in China.

Chapter 8 The "Chinese Way" Of Developing A Supply Base

Developing reliable and cost-efficient suppliers is not an easy task. I will show you here some good and some not-sogood experiences you may encounter while building and developing your Supply Base in China. However, if you are part of, or represent a large corporation with an extensive budget, then this information may make you chuckle, as with money, many of my struggles could have been avoided. **With unlimited funds at your disposal, you would hire consultants for every detail, and you would follow a very standard and safe route to building your China business.** Your end goal of having a presence in China, may it be for manufacturing, distribution, and/or sales, could be achieved without much interference from external forces if the availability of money is not an issue. Money goes a long way in China, and if you compare your China business with your current operation from your home country, you might be satisfied with the savings achieved. **However, if money is in short supply, let's examine how you can consider building a China presence for your business. When you try to build a company on a shoestring budget, every dollar spent or saved will be crucial to your success.** You will have to recognize quickly if any decision you make is in your best interest or if it simply satisfies your "business advisor." **The end result must be a quick return on your investment, as in China, the business climate and Government rules could change at a moment's notice and you should always be prepared with an exit strategy, just in case your plans don't work out.** You will be bombarded with "good advice" from many sources and the few **Englishspeaking Chinese you will meet will be out to impress you. Of course, their endgame is getting your trust, and for that matter, mostly your money.** They will try to convince you to hire their friends for all kinds of functions and eventually, you start depending on a slew of people around you who have just one thing in mind, and this is making money. **Westerners**

are known to have money and once you are committed, it is not easy to turn back. **You will be told over and over again that you have to play the benefit game and that everybody is doing it and it is part of doing business the "Chinese Way."** To a certain degree, this is true for small gift exchanges between business partners but stay away from long-term financial business arrangements which are not officially accounted for as it could lead to corruption and even blackmail. **Never forget that China is a tightly controlled Society**, and most Westerners are very inexperienced, and to a certain degree naïve, to understand the meaning of this and how it might affect their business. A suggestion of benefits to the wrong person may have dire consequences and can be used against you and stop you from achieving your goal. Do never forget that your competitors are watching you closely as well and they would love to catch you in an illegal act and get you banned for doing business in China. Do not believe that money spent on gifts and presents will lead you to the Garden of Eden, but it will help to get your business partners loosening up and you will notice quickly that the atmosphere is getting more informal. **Remember that in order to build a genuine friendship with your Chinese connections, it is of utmost importance to understand the basic Chinese ethics which makes it clearly understood that friendship comes before business.**

You will need a solid management team around you, and I suggest you do most interviews yourself and have an interpreter with you to navigate any misunderstandings. I have interviewed hundreds of Chinese for various positions from Production Manager, Sales, Office, and Accounting Personnel. I also got involved in getting to know production supervisors and quality control staff. Remember to always greet new employees with a smile and make them feel welcome at your place of work. **Your Supply Base can make or break your business, as quality control and not just low pricing will make your business a success.** Always visit your suppliers at their production plants and not just in their offices. Walk with them through the plant and observe the workers and see if there is tension between the machine operators and supervisors. Ask to talk to see the quality department and ask to see production reports and look around if you find scrap bins. This will give you quickly a great insight into how the quality is controlled. If you find scrap parts, take one and ask what went wrong with that part and how they can ensure that the part does not get passed on to the customer. You will be amazed by the excuses you will hear, and you will get a feel for their company and if you can rely on this supplier. I once had a supplier of foam parts and the shipment had many parts with ripped ends. Our quality department rejected the shipment and we contacted the supplier to replace the shipment. We got a quick reply from the supplier, that a partner of their business has decided that they will refuse to do business with us in the future since we are so picky and rejected their parts. I went to see the supplier and asked for a meeting with the owners. The parts were essential for our production, and the price was substantially lower than their competitors. I wanted to maintain our relationship. I suggested that we sort the parts from the rejected shipment, and they simply would replace the damaged parts and I would absorb the sorting costs. We had a nice dinner together and I asked them to quote me the extra costs if he would examine every part for any future shipments. He quoted a minimal increase, and he was a reliable supplier ever since. Sometimes it takes very little to get out of a difficult situation and the win-win principle can be applied to any negotiation tactic. In the next chapter, we will look at the development of a business relationship.

Chapter 9 How To Build Long-Lasting Business Relationships

When thinking and talking about China, Westerners must understand that any preconceived notion of China could be or actually is a falsification. China is infinitely more complex a place than can be imagined or understood by just reading a book. Here are some cultural hiccups that may be helpful to know about before you consider a business trip and how to avoid them. Don't forget to bring along those bi-lingual business cards.

1.   **The concept of time:** The definition of time in China does not necessarily designate when one hour gives way to the next. For example, at noon, to a Westerner, it is clearly at 12 PM, but for many Chinese, it could be a two-hour period from 11 a.m. to 1 p.m. Always be clear about what timeframe you're talking about.

2.   **Mistaking loud voices as a sign of hostility:** The Chinese speak several decibels higher than is common or even comfortable for Westerners, but this does not mean that they are upset or arguing.

3.   **Misconstruing Chinese displays of Greetings:** Shaking hands comes naturally to Westerners, but it is not always a comfortable practice for the Chinese, who in general, consider a handshake as impolite. However, now most Chinese will offer a weak handshake and they look a little reserved during their greetings. Do not be offended by this.

4.   **The importance of business cards exchanging before meetings:** A double-sided Western business card with simplified Chinese on one side is the first indication of respect toward your Chinese counterpart. Not having double-sided business cards is not unlike refusing to shake hands at the start of a Western business meeting. Even if you are familiar with the title and position of the person to whom you have been introduced, study his card, and then deliberately place it within clear sight in front of you on the table when you are sitting down.

5.   Not understanding the term "Guanxi": "Guanxi" is not easily translated into a single word that mirrors its meaning. "Relationships or connections outside the family" is the closest one might come to the meaning of what is at the very core of Chinese society and culture. It is, therefore, of utmost importance for the Chinese to get to know the person or people with whom they wish to conduct business before the business is conducted.

For a business to be conducted successfully, remember that The How and the Why, and the When, all rest on these relationships.

6.   Thinking a meal in China is just a meal: During your stay in China, on many occasions, you will most likely be invited to share a lunch or dinner. **However, during the meal, it will be considered rude to discuss any business.**

But that does not mean the meal isn't without a business goal in mind and remember what guanxi is all about. Don't be surprised if people who have not been to any of the business meetings you have attended appear at the dining table. There is usually no introduction and they simply sit down and leave quietly when the meal is over.

7.   Forgetting table etiquette: Many Chinese believe that luck is brought with good table manners and bad table manners will result in shame. From a Western perspective, there is always too much food on the table, but it is a sign of the host's prosperity. Always try each dish and especially be sure to accept the serving of what the host points out as the best dish, which he proudly offers to you as a sign of his hospitality.

8.   Passing on a toast: What fails to happen can matter as much as what happens and declining anything from one's host in China, even with a seemingly legitimate excuse, throws gloom over a meal. If you don't wish to drink, make your excuses early, before the toasts begin. Medical excuses are usually the most acceptable reason for declining a toast.

9.   Taking probing questions as an insult: The Chinese's total lack of inhibition can be the refreshing opposite of our politically correct approach to conversation. It turns out that the Chinese are capable of asking questions of what most people would want to know, and they are not afraid to ask about details of your private life. Be prepared for the social conversation that is often stunningly taboo-free. If you are a man, you might be asked about your financial assets; if you are a woman, you will undoubtedly be asked about your marital status.

10.   Never forget that dignity trumps money: Friendships are based on trust and mutual understanding. Don't get frustrated if you feel that your approach is not working, as there could be some reasons, which are most likely out of your control. **Always keep smiling and don't show your anxiety** as it might translate negatively towards your business partner.

My final observations and conclusions of my time spent in China

Communication is the key to understanding the cultural differences between the past and present within China. **Remember that listening and acceptance are more important than what any China expert can or will tell you**.

What works in Shanghai may not work in Beijing and certainly will be totally different in Jilin or Xiamen or Shenzhen, and when I say works, I mean the way you approach a business start-up, and your negotiations with the local government and communist party officials. **Each area of China has its own characteristics, and you need to get a feel for each area and adapt your thinking accordingly**. When talking to your Chinese friends, you will hear a lot of sayings. These could stem from Confucius to Tao to Mao. Many sayings are based on Buddhism or any other Chinese philosophy, but the most important part is the fact that you **try to understand and appreciate the wisdom behind the many sayings without prejudice or disregard**. Do not offer interpretations or try to show similarities to Western ways of thinking, simply accept what you hear and show your appreciation for your friendship.

General and Basic Business Practices for Success in China

As mentioned earlier, I like to highlight some of the basic requirements for you to consider before your final decision on your expansion plans.

Following is a list of the most important areas which require your utmost attention, and I will comment on these areas in detail for you to consider.

- **Activity-Based Costing System**
- **Chinese Lawyer**
- **Translator**
- **Government regulations**
- **Labor relations**
- **Management Team**
- **Banking**
- **Financial Statements**
- **Audits in China**

It is of utmost importance that you know your current costs and that you have a good basis to evaluate the costs of manufacturing in China. It will help you to weigh the benefits of moving your production to China.

You most likely have in your current manufacturing business a well-developed costing system, but just to be sure. I will suggest adjusting your costing system to an Activity Based System which can be useful in China to let you quickly compare the advantages and disadvantages of doing business in China.

Activity-Based Costing System

Basic Definitions of general accounting terms: Gross margin: Selling price less Direct Materials, Sub-components, and direct labor gross **profit:** Gross margin less Indirect labor, fringe benefits, and manufacturing overheads.

Bill of Material (BMO): the BMO will be used as the basis for raw materials, sub-components/services, direct labor, and carrying costs. **Raw Materials:** this represents the cost of raw materials purchased in bulk form and used in the manufacturing production of the product. **Sub-components:** this represents the costs of outside purchased components and service fees. **Carrying costs:** this represents the markup of materials and sub-components for expenses such as handling/storage/ interest. These costs can fluctuate between 3%-10% which you can base on historical costs. **Labor cost:** this is the actual hourly rate per employee for a particular work center. **The Burden Rate per hour is made up of the following: Manufacturing Overheads:** summarize the actual costs for fixed and variable overheads and divide by the annual hours, which are calculated based on shifts per day/week at 8 hours/ shifts. **Machine/Work Centre:** costs are based on total assets divided by several work centers based on lifetime hours, and it will give you the Machine/Work Centre cost per hour. **Floor space:** this is the sum of rent, property taxes, and insurance. It gives you an estimate of the total square feet of floor space used for manufacturing. You assign the devoted manufacturing activity occupied by the actual footage occupied by each work center which will give you the actual cost of the space used per machine/work center. **Other costs:** Costs that need to be divided into your work center cost include utilities, repairs and maintenance, and general factory expenses. **Fringe Benefits**: This includes indirect labor, benefits, and overtime costs. **Fixed non-manufacturing expenses:** this represents the cost of selling, general and administrative expenses (S.G.& A.) including interest incurred concerning the company's operating line.

When you have a good understanding of your current cost structure, you can now estimate the cost of manufacturing in China with the same assumptions of productivity but substitute the hourly costs with the Chinese labor and consider the carrying costs, including transportation and managerial costs. There might be a benefit also on your raw materials and sub-contract expenses. Once you analyze the new cost structure, you can quickly see if a move to China makes sense.

Lawyer

Once you have decided to make the move to China and you have decided on a location, now is the time to look for a lawyer near the area you decided upon, and a local lawyer will help you get the governmental applications and approvals.

It is most important you find a local business-oriented lawyer with experience dealing with foreign entities. If you are looking for a lawyer within a prestigious law firm or a lawyer who is recommended by your current lawyer, it will be very expensive and very frustrating, as they will assign a junior lawyer to your case, and only on face-to-face meetings you will meet the senior lawyer and most of the time they are situated in the large cities and do not understand the local issues which you will face. I advise you to ask around your local business community for companies who do manufacturing in China and ask them which lawyers they use in China. You will be amazed to find out the stories you will hear. Ideally, you find someone who deals with small clients and who has clients in different parts of China and Asia. I also advise you to employ a lawyer who knows the local area and has contacts within the Communist party and the governmental labor department, wherever your manufacturing base is located, and good connections to the local police commissioner will be helpful.

Translator

Now it is time to ask your lawyer for a reliable translator. Ideally, your translator should be someone who has business experience, has worked with foreign manufacturing entities, and has a good English understanding. It is important that the translator understands your questions and remarks and can convey your thoughts to the Chinese counterpart. Do not rely on the translator which is provided by the people who arranged the meeting. Always have your own translator in any meeting present. I remember one meeting, where my translator and the translator from my business JV partner started a big argument, and finally, the JV translator told my translator to stop being on the "White Mans" side as they are both Chinese and they should look after the benefits of the Chinese first. After I was able to come to a good conclusion with my JV partner, the translator who worked for him walked out of the meeting and refused to attend any further meetings.

When observing the conversations between your translator and the other party, you will be amazed when you ask a simple one-line question and then it follows a 5-minute discussion in Chinese, and you see tempers moving on both sides and all you needed was a simple yes or no answer. The best way to calm everyone down is to ask what plans have been made for dinner and you will be surprised how quickly you will get things done.

Government regulations and requirements

Your lawyer will arrange all the governmental applications and will arrange meetings in order for you to familiarize yourself with the local rules and regulations. You will quickly learn to meet all the different departments which need to approve your start-up of production. Never fail to mention any special occasion you are planning and politely mention that attendance at special dinners is appreciated. Always mention that you are in China to benefit the local people in China and that you are aware of the benefits doing business in China will have for you and your business at home.

Labor relations

Now is the time to find a Chinese manager who will represent you and negotiate with the labor union representatives and, if possible, meet also with a local Communist party representative. The more people you meet and openly tell them your intentions, you will quickly find ways to speed up any approval process. Always stress the benefits you bring to the community and the local economy stressing the fact of job creation.

Management Team

Based on your business at home, you will need to hire a solid management team. You will need a Production Manager and Office/Accounting Manager who speak English and who have experience dealing with Western companies. Depending on how you get your candidates for the jobs, either through referrals from an employment agency, always interview the candidates yourself and only hire them if you feel comfortable with them. You will also need to consider who in your current company will be the liaison between your current operation and the manufacturing set-up in China. Most likely, you will have some current employees spending some time in China for the manufacturing set-up and training of the Chinese employees.

Banking

Your current bank will most likely have a preference with which bank you should deal with in China, but if your manufacturing is in an outlying area, you will be better off dealing with one of the few larger local banks as long they can transfer money smoothly between China and your country. It is sometimes easier to get foreign transfer approvals with local banks, as they know all the ins and outs of the regulations and they have usually good relations with the authorities in charge of the approvals. The banking manager who will be assigned to you will be also a great benefit in general banking and auditing procedures. He will also be an extra eye on your general office personnel and procedures.

Financial Statements

Your Chinese accountant will need a basic understanding of your business practices in your homeland, and this will help him to set up an accounting system similar to your home setup. It is important that you are aware of any differences in accounting which might adjust the basic calculations in the profitability of your expansion plans. After the first few months of operating, have your home accountant take a look at the setup and have him understand any differences and adjustments needed. Also, depending on the corporate set-up you have chosen, there are tax implications to be considered, especially if you are in a Joint Venture position.

Audits in China

Your current auditor may have connections to a Chinese auditing firm and will advise you to make arrangements with the Chinese auditor. There are many financial reports needed within China for the Chinese authorities, and it is best to let the Chinese auditor decide how to complete all governmental requirements. Your Chinese lawyer will also be a good source to guide you in finding a suitable auditing firm.

This all said, I simply want you to be aware of the different steps needed to start your manufacturing place in China. There is no sure way to succeed, but good preparations for a start-up business in China will go a long way to get you the results you expect and desire.

Ask yourself one more time:

Why set up your Manufacturing Business in China?

After reading my various experiences, ask yourself this one question one more time and think about all that can go wrong with your expansion plans. Did you consider all the necessary steps for a successful start-up in China?

There are many reasons to move your manufacturing business to China:

The main reason is the basic cost advantage of manual labor. If your production requires mostly manual labor versus automation, your labor cost will be at an incredible advantage against your current costs and the costs of your local competitors. However, I strongly encourage you to be sure you know your bottom line and there is no better way than to implement an **Activity Based Costing System.** Know your costs and consider all factors, like the volume of your production, as transportation on low volume will eat into any advantage you gained with the low-cost production. Volumes must justify overseas production, and depending on your product, you might also find opportunities to sell your products in China and other Asian markets.

What form of a foreign manufacturing plant should you consider?

Wholly Owned Business?   Joint-Venture (JV)?   SubContract?

Each of these business structures has advantages and unfortunately, also disadvantages. Based on your decision, you will have to consider **Government regulations, Labor relations, and General HR issues.** Other basic issues to consider are your **Banking set-up, Financial Statements, and Audits in China, which have to be acceptable in your home country. Of course, you need a knowledgeable lawyer based in China who understands your business and who will look after the basic Government requirements.**

The trigger to decide to expand to China is no longer wild ambition or a big dream. It is a pure necessity as the 21st century is going to be the Asian century. It becomes a must to increase your market share in that region and China is the big fish. The decision to go to China cannot be taken lightly and you need to be willing to learn and adapt and commit to a serious budget which is needed to transform your business to include China in your go-forward plans.

Study and analyze the requirements as mentioned in my detailed descriptions in my last chapter on **General and Basic Business Practices in China.** You will be able to make your expansion decision into China based on facts and common understanding and not just on smart sales agents and consultants who know it all. Remember that they will not take any responsibility beyond their commissions, and they won't worry about what happens to your company after their initial sales presentation. You are the one who must be convinced that you made the right decision, a decision which is based on all the various facts presented to run a successful business out of China.

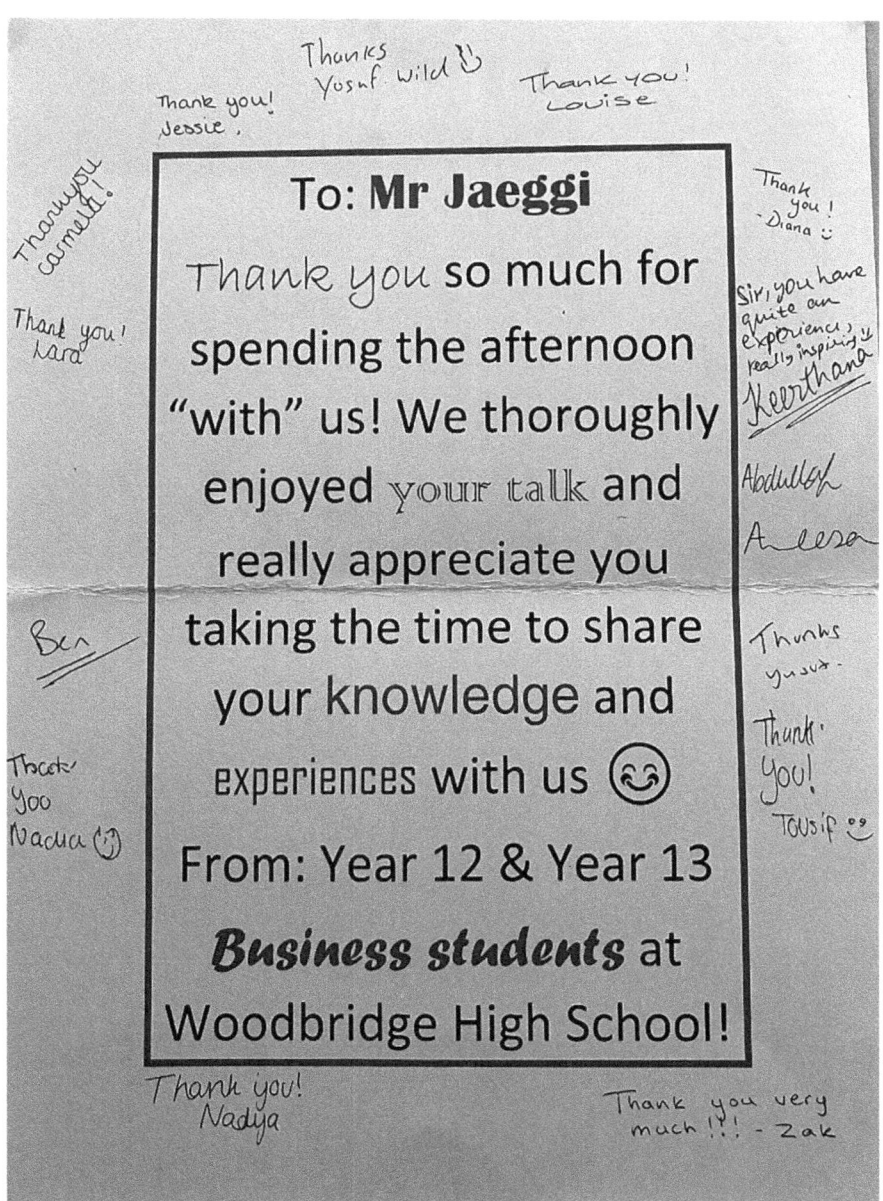

Thanks Yusuf Wild

Thank you! Jessie.

Thank you! Louise

Thankyou! carmulti.

Thank you! Lara

Thank you! Diana

Sir, you have quite an experience, really inspiring. Keerthana

Abdullah

Aleesa

Ben

Thank You Nadua

Thanks yusuf.

Thank You! Tousip

Thank you! Nadija

Thank you very much!! - Zak

To: Mr Jaeggi

Thank you so much for spending the afternoon "with" us! We thoroughly enjoyed your talk and really appreciate you taking the time to share your knowledge and experiences with us 😊

From: Year 12 & Year 13 *Business students* at Woodbridge High School!

Business students from the UK express gratitude for everything they have learned about business from me.

ABOUT THE AUTHOR

George Jaeggi

Born and educated in Switzerland with a basic banking apprenticeship certificate (KV). After completing the compulsory basic training in the Swiss Army, I immigrated as a 19-year-old to Canada. Due to a lack of English knowledge, I worked for the first 4 years in many basic labor jobs, including 1 year at a logging camp on Vancouver Island, until I found my first office job at a division of Magna, where I eventually advanced to be a divisional controller. In the year 2000, I opened my consulting company, Halten Management Services, and I helped manufacturing companies with their expansion plans and established various manufacturing facilities in Canada and different parts of China. I have conducted business in most parts of Europe, North America, Mexico, China, Korea, and Japan.